BREADSPEED

Wonderful No-Knead Yeast Breads in Two Hours

Elma Schemenauer

Farland Press Inc.

Farland Press Inc.
92 Caines Avenue
Willowdale, Ontario
CANADA
M2R 2L3

Illustrations: Maureen Shaughnessy
Cover Photography: Robert S. Schemenauer
Typesetting: Jay Tee Graphics Ltd.

Printed and bound in Canada

0 9 8 7 6 5 4 3 2 1 0

Canadian Cataloguing in Publication Data
Schemenauer, Elma
   Breadspeed.

Includes index.
ISBN 0-921718-00-4

1. Bread. 2. Flour. 3. Yeast. I. Title.

TX769.S24 1988   641.8'15   C88-095073-0

Special thanks to my mother, Agatha Martens, and to my mother-in-law, Bernice Schemenauer, who taught me a lot about baking and about living.

Many thanks also to the following, who tasted the breads in this book and provided encouragement and good advice.

Amyra Braha
Elio Bucci
George Christoffer
Marilyn Christoffer
Nancy Christoffer
Sharon Ord Delisle
Peter Hanson
Sharilyn Hanson
Barbara Hehner
Eric Hehner

Sherry Kornblum
Mary Macchiusi
Virginia Maxwell
Patricia Meier
Lynn Patterson
Jack Power
Judy Lynn Simpson
Robert Simpson
Richard Tanabe

Contents

PART I

PART II

A Personal Note from the Author

Confessions of a Lifelong Breadmaker

As a member of a wheat-growing Mennonite family, I grew up with breadbaking. Once a week the heady aroma of *bulki* (white bread) and *zwieback* (buns) would waft through our prairie farmhouse. My mother's chewy, nut-brown wholewheat bread was my special favorite.

I was about 11 when I baked my first batch of bread all by myself. I tested the lukewarm water on my wrist to make sure it was the right temperature for starting the yeast. I set the sponge. I kneaded the dough. I waited patiently through the hours-long first and second risings.

However, I'm not going to explain any of those time-honored techniques in this book. The reason? I've developed a brand-new method of breadmaking. It produces the same delicious results that my Mennonite mother, aunts, and grandmothers turned out. But in my method there's no second-guessing about water temperature. There's absolutely no kneading. And there are no long waiting periods.

Making bread the old-fashioned way takes about six hours. Using my BREADSPEED method, it takes two hours or less including cleanup. During most of that time, you aren't working at breadbaking either. You're relaxing or going about your other activities while your bread takes care of itself.

As a student and during my early working years, I had a couple of jobs in commercial bakeries. There I

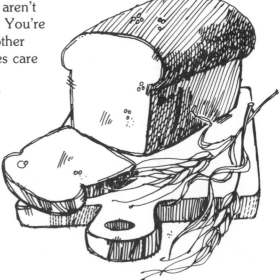

learned a lot about how various baking ingredients work. I also learned about kneading machines and other machines for baking.

However, I'm not going to talk much about machines in this book. My simple BREADSPEED method doesn't require machines beyond those found in the most ordinary kitchen. Of course, if you do have a food processor, blender, microwave, or other specialized machines, you can use them with this method if you wish — but they're not necessary. I'll say more about that in the section titled Equipment for BREADSPEED Baking.

How did I develop the BREADSPEED method? "By trial and error" is the short answer to that question. As a busy big-city writer, editor, and homemaker, I didn't always have time to bake bread the old-fashioned way. I started wondering if there was an easier method.

My work as a freelance editor inspired me to start experimenting.

From the mid-1980s on, people have been asking me to edit a lot of books on scientific topics.

All this science editing got me started researching the science behind breadbaking. "What is yeast, really?" I asked myself. "How does it grow? Is there a way to make yeast grow faster than it does in traditional bread-making? Do some types of flour respond better than others to the rising power of yeast?"

Through reading, lots of tryouts, good advice from my many patient tasters, and a lifelong interest in breadbaking, I've arrived at some answers to these questions. I want to share them with you in this book. Few joys in life can match the satisfaction of taking a perfectly browned loaf out of the oven for the enjoyment of those you love.

I wish you joy and love in BREADSPEEDING.

Elma Schemenauer
September 1988

Ingredients for
BREADSPEED Baking

Power Flour

"Kneading develops the gluten," said my mother, explaining to me as a child why we needed to knead and knead. . .and knead our bread dough. Gluten, formed when wheat-flour proteins absorb water, is what gives bread dough its elasticity—its bounce.

Years later, remembering Mom's explanation, I stood in a bulk food store, staring at a bin of gluten flour. The label said, "Gluten flour is high in protein and low in fat. Add to baked goods as a nutritional supplement."

Could gluten flour be used for more than a nutritional supplement? I wondered. If the reason for kneading is to develop gluten, why not add gluten straight to the dough and save all that time and fist power? As it turned out, my hunch was right, and gluten flour became the power flour of the BREADSPEED method.

The recipes in this book tell you how to use gluten flour, the power flour, to help take the work out of breadbaking. You'll be using gluten flour along with other types of flour. The following chart lists a variety of flours and describes their main characteristics.

A Bouquet of Flours

gluten flour	The power flour of the BREADSPEED method. Also a nutritional supplement high in protein and low in fat.
all-purpose flour	A blend of hard and soft milled wheats, suited to many baking needs. Specified as the white flour in BREADSPEED recipes because of its easy availability and reliable results.
unbleached flour	Has no preservatives or bleaching chemicals. May be used instead of all-purpose flour in any BREADSPEED recipe. However, results will be somewhat heavier, coarser in texture, and darker in color.
hard wheat flour	Ideally, hard wheat flour should be used in breadmaking. However, the quality of hard wheat flour available to the home baker is not as reliable as that of all-purpose flour. If you find a hard wheat flour that gives the results you want, use it. If not, use all-purpose flour.
wholewheat flour	Contains the whole wheat kernel including most of the bran and germ.
graham flour	Interchangeable with wholewheat, but usually a bit coarser.
buckwheat flour	Most often used for pancakes. Small amounts may be added to yeast breads for additional nutrition and flavor.
rye flour	Contains much less gluten than wheat flours, and is therefore commonly used in combination with them. In Europe in the past, the low price of rye and high price of wheat led to development of many delicious, nutritious rye breads still enjoyed today.

oat flour	Can be added in small amounts to most yeast doughs for more nutrition and flavor. You can easily make it by whirling dry rolled oats or oatmeal in a blender.
barley flour	Can be added in small amounts to most yeast doughs for more nutrition and flavor.
soy flour	Rich source of protein. Sold in low-fat and high-fat forms, interchangeable in recipes. The Cornell Formula, developed at New York's Cornell University, recommends increasing nutritional value of all-purpose flour by adding a tablespoon each of soy flour, wheat germ, and dry milk powder to each cup of flour used.
stone ground flour	Any of a variety of grains may be ground between stones rather than between metal rollers. Many people believe stone ground flours are more nutritious. Since they are coarser and heavier than other flours, you'll probably need about twice as much yeast when baking with stone ground flours.

You can usually buy the more common flours in a grocery or supermarket. If you can't find the flours you want there, try a bulk food store or health food store. If you have access to a flour mill, you may be able to obtain a variety of flours directly from the mill.

Good cooking is not only friend, wife and lover,
But playmate, hobby, craft, encounter group, and psychotherapist.
— William Rice

Seeds, Meals, and Other Found-ins

One of the big advantages of baking your own bread is that you can easily include ingredients that will make it much more nutritious than many commercial breads. As we've seen, using highly nutritious flours is one way of

doing this. Another way is to add what I call "found-ins." These include various seeds, nuts, and meals. (A meal differs from a flour in that it is much coarser, and does not react with the yeast as most bread flours do.)

Since found-ins don't react with yeast, you can add reasonable amounts of them to any BREADSPEED recipe. For example, in a recipe calling for 2-1/2 cups (600 mL) flour, you could easily add 1/2 cup (120 mL) *each* of cracked wheat, cornmeal, and sunflower seeds. Too great a volume of found-ins, though, may result in bread that is too heavy or dry.

Also note that, when you add greater amounts of found-ins than those called for in a BREADSPEED recipe, you increase the amount of dough so that it may no longer fit into the size of pan specified. A loaf, when put into its pan, should fill only about 2/3 of that pan. If, when forming your loaf, you see that it is bigger than that, you can simply use a bigger pan. Another solution is to use the extra dough to make a few rolls.

Following is a list of found-ins you could consider for your breads.

cracked wheat	anise seeds (small amounts)
cornmeal	
oatmeal	caraway seeds (small amounts)
rye meal	
barley meal	dill seeds (small amounts)
wheat germ	
bran	flax seeds (cure for constipation)
raisins	
sunflower seeds	chopped peanuts (or other nuts)
sesame seeds	
poppy seeds	

Forms of Yeast

One thing that gives breadbaking such a gut-level appeal in our high-tech age is that we raise breads with something that is very much alive—yeast—rather than with cold harsh chemicals such as baking powder and baking soda. Yeast cells are so small we can't see them. However, they are in fact tiny plants that we "cultivate" and cooperate with during the process of bread-making.

To be sure, if you've tried other breadbaking methods and been disappointed, you might think of yeast cells as "yeast beasts" to be tamed, rather than as friendly, cooperative little helpers. With the BREADSPEED method, I think you'll be pleasantly surprised. Your yeast will work well for you again and again, producing feast after feast for your admiring family and friends.

Yeast for baking is commonly available in three forms, any of which works in the BREADSPEED method.

Back of the loaf is the snowy flour,
And back of the flour the mill,
And back of the mill is the wheat and the shower,
And the sun and the Father's will.
— Maltbie Davenport Babcock

active dry yeast	Composed of beadlike granules. Recommended as the yeast in BREADSPEED recipes because it is more readily available and keeps better than compressed yeast. I also recommend it over fast-rising or "instant" yeast because the active dry yeast results in bread with better aroma, flavor, texture, and keeping quality.
fast-rising yeast	Finer, more irregularly shaped granules than active dry yeast. Produces quite satisfactory results when used according to the BREADSPEED method. However, when fast-rising yeast is mixed directly into the dry ingredients as some methods suggest, I have found the bread has poorer aroma, flavor, texture, and keeping quality.
compressed yeast	Comes in moist cubes usually wrapped in foil. Grayish-tan, but may be a little brown at the edges. Produces excellent results, but is not as readily available as other yeasts. Also does not keep as well.

Refrigerate your yeast to keep it fresh. If you're not sure it's fresh enough to use, dissolve a sample of it in water as described at the beginning of any BREADSPEED recipe. (In the case of compressed yeast, simply crumble it into the water with your fingers.) If, after 10 to 20 min, your yeast mixture has a foamy "head," go ahead and use it.

You can buy yeast in foil envelopes or, in the case of compressed yeast, in foil-wrapped cubes. If you're planning to do any amount of baking, I recommend buying it in bulk instead. Jars, cans, or plastic bags of yeast may be available in a grocery or supermarket. If not, try a bulk food store or health food store. Equivalent measures are as follows.

1 Tbsp. (15 mL) dry yeast =
1 envelope dry yeast =
1 cube compressed yeast.

Vitamin Magic

This brings us to the vitamin magic part of BREADSPEED baking. In several bread books over a number of years, I had noticed timid references to adding vitamin C to bread dough to aid rising. Most references, however, seemed sketchy, as if the method wasn't effective or hadn't been well worked out.

Since I had several kinds of vitamin C (ascorbic acid) tablets around the house, it wasn't hard for me to start experimenting. I found that most forms of vitamin C, either powder or tablets crushed to a powder, produce somewhat satisfactory fast-rising bread.

Head and shoulders above all the others, though, is calcium ascorbate powder. This is a vitamin C supplement that has been combined with calcium to make it non-irritating to people whose stomachs can't take the acidity of other vitamin C supplements.

If you can't find calcium ascorbate powder among the vitamins on your drugstore shelves, ask a pharmacist, doctor, or health food store employee. If you can't find the powder, buy the tablets and use a mortar and pestle or other method to crush them to a fine powder.

Obtaining the calcium ascorbate powder and gluten flour are the two hardest things about BREADSPEED baking. The rest is ridiculously easy. And when you're eating that delicious bread created by your own hands, you'll know that, even if you had to hunt a bit for BREADSPEED's two magic ingredients, the search was well worth it.

Besides the ingredients already discussed, you don't need a whole lot more to make bread. The following chart discusses some of the other commonly used ingredients.

What hymns are sung, what praises said
For home-made miracles of bread?
— *Louis Untermeyer*

Other Major Bread Ingredients

water	Nothing complicated here. As we'll see, determining water temperature isn't as crucial in BREADSPEED baking as in the traditional method.
salt	I try to avoid salt as much as possible in cooking. However, it really is necessary in breads as it controls the action of the yeast. If you wish, instead of regular salt, you can use sea salt. It's not highly treated or refined, and is rich in minerals including iodine.
sweeteners	Except for the small amount used to help get the yeast started, you can leave out any sweeteners called for in BREADSPEED recipes. Also, in most, you can substitute molasses, honey, syrup, or brown sugar for any white sugar specified.
fats	The Mennonites of my childhood were never afraid to eat fats. But since most of them did a lot of hard physical work, they had a better chance of burning off the extra calories than people in sit-down jobs do today. Fats such as butter, margarine, shortening, and meat drippings enrich bread. They improve its color, texture, and keeping quality. Vegetable oil doesn't have quite the same improving effects, but you may wish to use it since it is more healthful. On the other hand, in most BREADSPEED recipes, you can simply omit fat altogether and still make satisfactory bread.
milk	Milk adds nutritional value, and enhances crust color and keeping quality. Most BREADSPEED recipes call for milk powder. You can use instant or non-instant, skim or whole milk powder. If you decide to use liquid milk, replace some or most of the recipe's water with it. The milk doesn't need to be scalded unless it's unpasteurized. However you should heat any milk used to the temperature of hot tap water.

Ingredients at Your Fingertips

Yeast, calcium ascorbate, most types of shortening, and flours for bread-making (other than all-purpose flour) should be stored in a cool dry place such as a refrigerator or cool dry basement. One way to help make bread-making easy is to pile all your refrigerated bread ingredients into one large plastic bag or other container. When you want to make bread, simply pull out the whole bag and set it on the kitchen counter. That way you'll have your ingredients at your fingertips.

All breadmaking ingredients should really be at room temperature before you begin mixing the dough. It's a good idea to measure the dry ingredients into the mixing bowl and let them warm up for a few minutes before proceeding. In the meantime you can put your bag of breadmaking ingredients back into the refrigerator.

Equipment for BREADSPEED Baking

A Low-Tech, Easy Cleanup Approach

Developing, testing, and retesting the recipes in this book has made me acutely aware of one point: Anything one can do to reduce dishwashing is a boon and a blessing. Even if you have a dishwasher, some breadbaking equipment is always either too big or too gucky to load into it.

Particularly troublesome to wash, I've found, are food processor and blender parts. Considering this and considering that not everybody has specialized kitchen machines, I've made the BREADSPEED method as low-tech as possible. Following is a list of what I consider basic equipment. In almost every case, you can improvise if you don't have the specified item.

Give us this day our daily bread.
— The Lord's Prayer

A. PLASTIC BOWL WITH VERTICAL SIDES. Rising bread should stay warm, and plastic holds warmth better than metal or glass. A plastic salad spinner bowl will do for small batches of bread. For large batches, try a plastic dishpan with high straight sides.

B. TWO LARGE, WIDE MEASURING CUPS. Use one for wet ingredients, the other for dry. Since you'll be starting your yeast right in the cup, it's a good idea to have a wide one. This gives the yeast more surface area on which to grow.

C. MEASURING SPOONS. If you don't have spoons specifically made for measuring, a soupspoon from your everyday collection of cutlery will do for a tablespoon (round it somewhat if it's smaller than a standard table-spoon). A dessert spoon should do for a teaspoon.

D. RUBBER SCRAPER. This is for scraping reluctant trickles of wet ingredients out of the measuring cup into the bowl.

E. LARGE MIXING SPOON—WOODEN OR METAL. If you have a food processor, you may want to use it to mix your dough. However, as I've said, I find it so much work to wash all the parts afterwards that I much prefer a spoon. Also, many food processors won't do much dough at a time, which is a disadvantage for larger batches of bread.

F. PLASTIC WRAP OR WAXED PAPER. If you have clean plastic bags saved from grocery shopping, you can cut these up and use them instead.

G. MINUTE TIMER. A timer may be part of your stove's standard equip-ment. If not, you can buy a portable one at a hardware. Or use a wrist-watch with an alarm.

H. COOKIE SHEET OR BAKE BOARD. To me, scrubbing a bake board seems a great chore. I find a cookie sheet just as good a surface for shaping loaves, and much easier to wash.

I. LARGE SHARP KNIFE. You'll

need this for cutting off pieces of dough when making rolls or several loaves at a time. If it has serrated edges and isn't too thick, you can also use it to slice that beautiful bread once you've created it.

J. PLANT MISTER. The BREAD-SPEED method includes spraying your loaves with water once they're formed. An inexpensive sprayer made for misting plants will do the job. Or you can just sprinkle on small drops of water with your fingers.

K. BAKING PANS. A loaf of bread, when first put into its baking pan, should fill about 2/3 of that pan. This allows for just enough rising to make a lovely high loaf. If you keep this rule in mind, you can use a variety of metal pans for breadbaking. You'll generally obtain the best results with loaf-shaped pans for bread. If you use quarry tiles under them (see page 20), then the cheapest of bargain basement pans will do. However, it's best not to use glass pans or disposable aluminum foil ones.

All BREADSPEED bread recipes are designed to fit pans of the following dimensions (measured from the top of the pan).

8-1/2 in. long by 4-1/2 in. wide by 2-1/2 in. deep (22 cm long by 12 cm wide by 6 cm deep)

For rolls, a cookie sheet will do. However, rolls rise better in a pan with sides about 2 in. (5 cm) high.

L. OVEN. Best results are achieved with an ordinary oven; that is, an electric, gas, coal, or wood-heated oven. It is possible to bake bread in a microwave oven, but the crust will not brown. Combination ovens, which use both convection heat and microwave energy, do color the crust, but not much. To offset the problem of pale crusts on breads baked in a micro-wave, you can use a variety of toppings: for example, cracked wheat, poppy seeds, icing. All BREADSPEED

recipes assume the use of a conventional (not microwave) oven.

M. POT HOLDERS AND METAL SPATULA. These are for taking your bread out of the oven and out of the pans.

N. UNGLAZED QUARRY TILES. Julia Child, James Beard, and other noted chefs recommend using unglazed quarry tiles for baking French bread. I've found tiles good for that, and also for any other loaves on which you want a substantial, well browned crust. An added benefit is that, because the tiles hold the heat, you use less energy to maintain baking temperature.

For the average home oven, you'll need about 8 square tiles approximately 5-3/4 in. (15 cm) on a side. You can buy them at almost any flooring tile store or building supply center that sells ceramic tiles.

Place your oven rack at its middle position or one notch higher or lower (a little experimenting will tell you which position works best in your particular oven). Then simply lay the tiles side by side on top of the rack. You don't need to cover the rack's entire surface. In fact, you should leave at least 2 in. (5 cm) all around the edge to let the heat circulate.

When you're ready to put your pans of bread in the oven, simply set them straight on the tiles. With tiles, you can bake crusty, evenly browned loaves in the flimsiest, cheapest pans (but of course you can use better pans if you have them). Just one caution: Tiles don't seem well suited to rolls or very sweet breads, as they can make the bottoms brown too quickly. Simply take the tiles out when you bake these.

The BREADSPEED Method

Amazingly Simple and Astonishingly Delicious

I've kept the instructions for BREADSPEED recipes deliberately simple. That's to avoid having you

Borscht and bread make your cheeks red.
— Jewish proverb

standing in the kitchen with a yeasty spoon in your hand, reading and reading. . .and reading. However, since the BREADSPEED method is unconventional, you'll probably want a fuller explanation the first time you try it.

The following Basic Bread recipe uses only the absolutely essential ingredients—no frills such as shortening, milk powder, or sweeteners. Once you've made Basic Bread, letting the detailed instructions walk you through the process, you'll be ready to go BREADSPEEDING with the more streamlined recipe instructions in the rest of this book.

By the way, Basic Bread, though basic, is absolutely delicious. So prepare for rave reviews from your loved ones or anyone else lucky enough to be standing by waiting to try it. This recipe makes one loaf.

Basic Bread

imperial units		metric units
1/2 Tbsp.	sugar	7 mL
1 Tbsp.	active dry or fast-rise yeast	15 mL
1/4 cup	cool or lukewarm water	60 mL
2 cups	all-purpose flour (or equal parts all-purpose and wholewheat flour)	480 mL
1/2 cup	gluten flour	120 mL
1 tsp.	salt or sea salt	5 mL
1/3 tsp.	calcium ascorbate powder	2 mL
1 cup	hot tap water	240 mL

"Nobody, my darling,
Could call me
A fussy man —
BUT
I do like a little bit of butter to my bread!"
— A.A. Milne, The King's Breakfast

A. GIVE THE YEAST A HEAD START. For this you need only two utensils, a tablespoon and a large wide measuring cup. Measure the sugar into the cup. With the same spoon, measure the yeast into the cup. Then pour in cool or lukewarm water just up to the 1/4 cup (60 mL)

measuring mark on the cup (no need to measure water before pouring it in).

More traditional methods recommend starting the yeast in water at about 110°F (43°C). Actually, cool water will do just as well, though the yeast action will be slightly slower. I find it much easier to just run cool water out of the tap, rather than second-guessing or using a thermometer to arrive at exactly the right lukewarm temperature. The most important thing is not to start the yeast in water that is too hot, since this will kill it.

Once you have the sugar, yeast, and water in the cup, give them a brief stir with the same tablespoon. Lumps don't matter. Set the yeast mixture in a warm, draft-free place till needed (10 to 30 min). If your kitchen is cool, cover the yeast mixture. Run some hot tap water into a bowl or sink and set the yeast in there to keep cosy.

B. MEASURE AND MIX THE DRY INGREDIENTS. With your second measuring cup and a teaspoon, measure the dry ingredients into a plastic mixing bowl, preferably a straight-sided one. If you've stored your ingredients in a cool place such as a refrigerator, let them warm up a few minutes at room temperature before proceeding.

C. MIX THE LIQUID AND DRY INGREDIENTS. The water you use at this point should be 120°F to 130°F (49°C to 54°C). I find that turning my hot water tap on and letting the water run till it's at its hottest works well. You may find the same. If you're doubtful, use a candy or meat thermometer to measure the temperature of your hot tap water the first time or two you bake bread. Water a bit hotter than 130°F (54°C) is still OK. However, take note:

Temperatures over 140°F (60°C) kill yeast. Mixing and rising must take place at temperatures lower than this.

Pour the hot tap water over the dry ingredients. Then, to take full advantage of the heat, *immediately* add the yeast mixture and mix *everything* together.

As I've indicated, I prefer a large wooden or metal spoon for mixing. However, if you wish, you can use a food processor or other suitable machine at this point. Mix thoroughly but don't knead. Dough will be a bit moister than in many traditional bread recipes.

Flours and humidities vary. Therefore you may need just a bit more hot tap water to allow all the dry ingredients to mix in fairly easily.

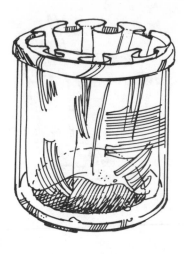

D. LET THE DOUGH RISE IN THE BOWL. Lay plastic wrap or waxed paper over the dough, touching the surface. This, together with the plastic bowl, helps hold in the warmth. Yeast doughs have a habit of "sulking" and not rising well if they're sitting in even a little draft. To prevent this, cover the bowl loosely with a lid or tea towel and set in a warm place as free of drafts as possible. (Don't cover tightly, as bubbles of carbon dioxide from the rising dough could cause the lid to "pop.")

Ideally bread dough should rise at 80°F to 85°F (27°C to 29°C). If your kitchen is cooler than this, use a method such as one of the following to keep the dough cosy.

• Run hot tap water into the sink. Set the bowl of dough into it. You may need to add a little more hot tap water during the rising period.

• If your kitchen is too cool, putting the dough upstairs may be all you need to do. Often an upstairs room is warmer than a main-floor kitchen.

• Note: For the following method, you *must* use a bowl made of material you know is safe for your microwave oven. Set the loosely covered bowl in a dish of hot water in the microwave. Turn the microwave on to medium for 1 min or low for 4 min. Then turn it off and leave for 5 to 15 min. If the dough hasn't at least doubled in bulk during this time, repeat the process.

No matter which raising method you use, your BREADSPEED dough should approximately double in bulk in 30 min. (In the traditional method, it takes an hour or longer.) One way to gauge if the dough has indeed doubled is to stick a piece of masking tape on the side of the bowl when you set the dough to rise. Stick the tape at the point where the dough should be when doubled. Then you can easily tell by looking, especially if your bowl is made of a somewhat see-through material.

If for some reason you can't take care of your dough after 30 min have passed, don't worry. BREADSPEED dough is remarkably adaptable to changes in schedule such as a surprise visit from your in-laws or a call to pick up your child at school. Except for the microwave method, you can leave the dough rising in the bowl for up to 2 hours without attention. After 2 hours, you can simply punch it down and let it rise again without doing any damage.

E. FORM THE LOAF. Peel off the plastic wrap or waxed paper. Turn the dough out onto a generously floured cookie sheet or board. With generously floured hands, pat the dough into a rectangular shape. (You can use a rolling pin, but I prefer fingers because they're easier to find and simpler to wash.)

Make the shorter sides of your dough rectangle about the same length as the longer sides of your loaf pan. Starting from one of the shorter sides, roll the dough up tightly like a jellyroll. When you get to the end, pinch the seam together with your fingers and then smooth it out as much as you can.

At each end of your loaf, push the side of your hand down to form a thin strip. Turn these strips under neatly, pinching their edges to seal them to the bottom of the loaf.

Brush the extra flour off the bottom and sides of the loaf. Using a plant mister or other method, spray the bottom and sides generously with water.

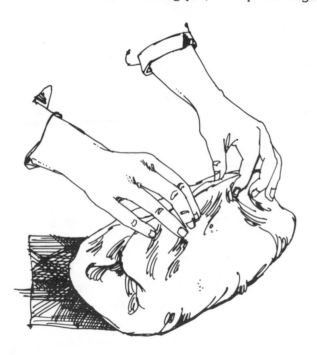

All sorrows are less with bread.
— Spanish proverb

F. PUT THE LOAF INTO THE PAN. Oil or grease the bottom and sides of the pan, and sprinkle them with a little yellow or white cornmeal. The cornmeal is not essential, but it gives a professional finish to your loaf and helps it slide out of the pan easily.

Turn your loaf topside up, lift it with both hands, and plop it into the pan. The loaf, as mentioned before, should take up about 2/3 of the space in the pan. If you're not satisfied with the smoothness or regularity of your loaf, you can pat and poke it at this stage to improve it. (After the loaf starts rising in the pan, however, you shouldn't touch it.) Spray the top of the loaf generously with water.

G. LET THE LOAF RISE IN THE PAN. If you're using quarry tiles as suggested on page 20, arrange them on an oven rack about halfway up in your oven. Make sure to leave at least a 2-in. (5-cm) space around the edge of the tiled area.

Set the pan onto the tiles (or bare rack if you're not using tiles). Turn the oven on to its *lowest* setting. In most ovens, this is about 85°F (29°C), which is just about right. If in doubt, use a thermometer to check how hot your oven is at its lowest setting. It can be a bit hotter than 85°F (29°C), but should definitely not be close to 140°F (60°C).

Leave the loaf in the oven at the lowest setting for 10 to 20 min, or until it has risen 1 to 2 in. (2.5 cm to 5.0 cm) above the top of the pan.

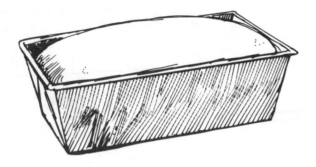

H. BAKE THE LOAF. With the loaf still in the oven, turn the temperature up to 400°F (200°C). As the oven heats up, the loaf will continue to rise for awhile. Then it will start baking. From the time of turning up the heat, your loaf should take 30 to 45 min to get done.

I. DETERMINING WHEN THE LOAF IS DONE. When the specified time is up, take the loaf out of the oven and use a metal spatula to tip it out of the pan. If the bottom and sides of the crust are an even, golden brown, the loaf is done. If not, simply plop it back into its pan and return it to the oven for a further 10 to 20 min.

Traditional bread recipes usually say a loaf is done when thumping produces a hollow sound. I've found that thumping a loaf at almost any stage of baking produces a sound I'd describe as hollow. Therefore I recommend the crust-checking method instead.

If you like a really brown, chewy crust, keep on baking the loaf, checking the bottom crust from time to time until it suits you. If during this process, you notice the top crust becoming too brown, turn down the heat or protect the top with an aluminum foil tent.

If you don't like your crust very brown and chewy, it's best not to use the quarry tiles. As soon as the minimum baking time is up, do your crust-checking as described above. Don't bake the loaf any longer than it takes to get the bottom and sides a pleasant golden brown. You can also keep the crust from being very chewy by brushing the loaf all over with butter or margarine as soon as it comes out of the oven.

J. COOLING, SLICING, AND KEEPING THE LOAF. You can slice the bread hot out of the oven. Though your slices may look a bit messy, this is of course the most delicious way to eat it.

If you prefer a more genteel approach, cool the loaf on a rack if you have one. After it has cooled, it will slice more neatly, either with a regular serrated knife or with an electric one.

Though BREADSPEED loaves don't include preservatives as many commercial loaves do, they are beautifully moist and don't dry out easily. They will keep well at room temperature, wrapped in plastic or waxed paper, for 4 to 5 days. (Make sure breads are thoroughly cooled before wrapping them.) In a refrigerator, BREADSPEED breads will easily keep for a week to 10 days. However, refrigeration does tend to harden any bread.

BREADSPEED breads freeze beautifully, either whole or sliced. Just put them in plastic bags or wrap them well with plastic wrap. You'll find that BREADSPEED breads keep their quality better than many commercial breads when frozen. One reason for this is that the ingredients you use when baking at home are generally of higher quality than those used in many commercial bakeries.

Think about it. Wouldn't you rather feed those higher quality, more nutritious ingredients to your family? That's a strong argument for baking your own bread. Fortunately, with the BREADSPEED method, it's fun, fast, and easy.

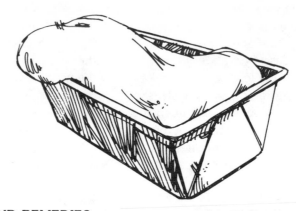

Troubleshooting Chart

Remedies for Less Than Perfect Breads

PROBLEMS	EXPLANATIONS AND REMEDIES
Poor volume, with close heavy texture.	Dough contained too much salt or did not rise long enough or was put in too large a pan. Next time control these factors more accurately.
Uneven texture with big holes in bread.	Some people consider this an advantage, especially with French and similar breads. If you feel the texture is too uneven and coarse, cut down on the rising time.
Loaf spreads too much over top of pan.	Either you stuffed in too much dough for the size of the pan or it rose too long. Dough, when put to rise in a loaf pan, should fill only 2/3 of that pan and should be allowed to rise only 1 or 2 in. above the top of the pan before the oven temperature is turned up.

Top of loaf is brown enough but sides and bottom are pale and soft.	Using quarry tiles as suggested on page 20 and/or baking bread on a lower oven rack should help prevent this. If you notice the problem when crust-checking for doneness, you can take the loaf out of its pan and finish baking it on quarry tiles if you have them in the oven, or on a cookie sheet. If top of loaf starts getting too brown, protect it with an aluminum foil tent and turn the heat down slightly.
Top of loaf creases and sags.	Probably there was too much liquid in the dough. The bread is likely to be good anyway, provided you make sure you bake it long enough.
Bread browns unevenly or rises more on one side than the other.	This can be caused by hot spots in your oven or an uneven distribution of heat due to having too many loaves baking at one time. Space the pans as evenly as possible in the oven. If there is room, set pans on an angle to promote better circulation of heat around them.
Lumps or colored streaks in the bread.	These are generally caused by not mixing the wet and dry ingredients thoroughly. Next time make sure to do so. If you're making a large batch of bread, you may have to set aside your trusty spoon and mix the dough with your hands. There's no need to knead it though. This is no-knead bread!
Bread is hard to get out of the pan.	The bread may not have been allowed to rise long enough in the pan. Another reason for sticking is not oiling or greasing the pan well enough. Make sure to do this thoroughly. A generous sprinkling of yellow or white cornmeal over the bottom and sides of the oiled or greased pan will also help the bread slide out more easily.

Standard White Bread / As with any BREADSPEED recipe, you can include soy flour and wheat germ to increase nutritive value. Don't worry about how they'll make white breads look or taste. In the amounts specified, they seem to simply "disappear."

3 loaves	1 loaf		1 loaf	3 loaves
1-1/2 Tbsp.	1/2 Tbsp.	sugar	7 mL	21 mL
3 Tbsp.	1 Tbsp.	active dry or fast-rise yeast	15 mL	45 mL
3/4 cup	1/4 cup	cool or lukewarm water	60 mL	180 mL
6 cups	2 cups	all-purpose flour	480 mL	1440 mL
1-1/2 cup	1/2 cup	gluten flour	120 mL	360 mL
3/8 cup	1/8 cup	soy flour (or less or omit)	30 mL	90 mL
1-1/2 cup	1/2 cup	wheat germ (or less or omit)	120 mL	360 mL
1-1/2 cup	1/2 cup	milk powder	120 mL	360 mL
3 tsp.	1 tsp.	salt or sea salt	5 mL	15 mL
2/3 tsp.	1/3 tsp.	calcium ascorbate powder	2 mL	4 mL
3/8 cup	1/8 cup	soft shortening or oil (or less or more)	30 mL	90 mL
3 cups	1 cup	hot tap water	240 mL	720 mL

1. Measure sugar into wide measuring cup. With same spoon, measure and add yeast.

2. Add cool or lukewarm water. Stir (lumps don't matter). Set in warm, draft-free place till needed (10 to 25 min).

3. Measure dry ingredients into plastic bowl. Mix well.

4. Add shortening and hot tap water to dry ingredients.

5. Immediately add yeast mixture and mix everything together very well with big spoon.

6. If some of the dry mixture won't mix in fairly easily, add a *little* more hot tap water.

7. Lay food wrap right over dough, touching surface. Cover bowl loosely. Set in warm, draft-free place.

8. After 30 min, dough should be about double in bulk. Peel off food wrap. Turn dough out on generously floured cookie sheet or board.

9. With generously floured hands, form loaf (or loaves).

10. Brush off extra flour. Spray bottom and sides of loaf with water.

11. Oil loaf pan. Set loaf in pan and spray top with water.

12. Set bread into oven and turn oven to its *lowest* setting. Leave 10 to 25 min.

13. When dough has risen 1 to 2 in. (2.5 to 5.0 cm) above top of pan, turn oven up to 400°F (200°C).

14. From time of turning heat up, bake 30 to 45 min or till sides and bottom are nicely browned.

"Bread," says he, "dear brothers, is the staff of life."
— Jonathan Swift

Potato Bread / *Mashed potato gives this bread a bouncy texture and a delicate, unique flavor.*

3 loaves	1 loaf		1 loaf	3 loaves
1-1/2 Tbsp.	1/2 Tbsp.	sugar	7 mL	21 mL
3 Tbsp.	1 Tbsp.	active dry or fast-rise yeast	15 mL	45 mL
3/4 cup	1/4 cup	cool or lukewarm water	60 mL	180 mL
6 cups	2 cups	all-purpose flour (or equal parts all-purpose and wholewheat flour)	480 mL	1440 mL
1-1/2 cup	1/2 cup	gluten flour	120 mL	360 mL
1-1/2 cup	1/2 cup	milk powder (or less or omit)	120 mL	360 mL
3 tsp.	1 tsp.	salt or sea salt	5 mL	15 mL
2/3 tsp.	1/3 tsp.	calcium ascorbate powder	2 mL	4 mL
3/8 cup	1/8 cup	soft shortening or oil (or less or omit)	30 mL	90 mL
3	1	medium potato(es) boiled in jacket, peeled, and thoroughly mashed	1	3
3	1	egg(s), slightly beaten	1	3
2 cups	2/3 cup	hot tap water	160 mL	480 mL

1. Measure sugar into wide measuring cup. With same spoon, measure and add yeast.

2. Add cool or lukewarm water. Stir (lumps don't matter). Set in warm, draft-free place till needed (10 to 25 min).

3. Measure dry ingredients into plastic bowl. Mix well.

4. Add mashed potato(es), slightly beaten egg(s), and hot tap water to dry ingredients.

5. Immediately add yeast mixture and mix everything together very well with big spoon.

6. If some of the dry mixture won't mix in fairly easily, add a *little* more hot tap water.

7. Lay food wrap right over dough, touching surface. Cover bowl loosely. Set in warm, draft-free place.

8. After 30 min, dough should be about double in bulk. Peel off food wrap. Turn dough out on generously floured cookie sheet or board.

9. With generously floured hands, form loaf (or loaves).

10. Brush off extra flour. Spray bottom and sides of loaf with water.

11. Oil loaf pan. Set loaf in pan and spray top with water.

12. Set bread into oven and turn oven to its *lowest* setting. Leave 10 to 25 min.

13. When dough has risen 1 to 2 in. (2.5 to 5.0 cm) above top of pan, turn oven up to 400°F (200°C).

14. From time of turning heat up, bake 30 to 45 min or till sides and bottom are nicely browned.

Cheese Bread / *All you need for a delicious meal is this hearty bread and a soup or salad. You can coarsely grate the cheese. Or for a more dramatic effect, just hack it into marble-sized chunks.*

3 loaves	1 loaf		1 loaf	3 loaves
1-1/2 Tbsp.	1/2 Tbsp.	sugar	7 mL	21 mL
3 Tbsp.	1 Tbsp.	active dry or fast-rise yeast	15 mL	45 mL
3/4 cup	1/4 cup	cool or lukewarm water	60 mL	180 mL
6 cups	2 cups	all-purpose flour (or equal parts all-purpose and wholewheat flour)	480 mL	1440 mL
1-1/2 cup	1/2 cup	gluten flour	120 mL	360 mL
1-1/2 cup	1/2 cup	milk powder	120 mL	360 mL
3 tsp.	1 tsp.	salt or sea salt	5 mL	15 mL
2/3 tsp.	1/3 tsp.	calcium ascorbate powder	2 mL	4 mL
3-3/4 cups	1-1/4 cup	coarsely grated or cut-up cheese — use one or more of these: sharp cheddar, Gruyère, Swiss Emmenthaler, sharp Colby	300 mL	900 mL
3 Tbsp.	1 Tbsp.	paprika	15 mL	45 mL
3 cups	1 cup	hot tap water	240 mL	720 mL

1. Measure sugar into wide measuring cup. With same spoon, measure and add yeast.

2. Add cool or lukewarm water. Stir (lumps don't matter). Set in warm, draft-free place till needed (10 to 25 min).

3. Measure dry ingredients into plastic bowl. Mix well.

4. Add hot tap water to dry ingredients.

5. Immediately add yeast mixture and mix everything together very well with big spoon.

6. If some of the dry mixture won't mix in fairly easily, add a *little* more hot tap water.

7. Lay food wrap right over dough, touching surface. Cover bowl loosely. Set in warm, draft-free place.

8. After 30 min, dough should be about double in bulk. Peel off food wrap. Turn dough out on generously floured cookie sheet or board.

9. With generously floured hands, form loaf (or loaves).

10. Brush off extra flour. Spray bottom and sides of loaf with water.

11. Oil loaf pan. Set loaf in pan and spray top with water.

12. Set bread into oven and turn oven to its *lowest* setting. Leave 10 to 25 min.

13. When dough has risen 1 to 2 in. (2.5 to 5.0 cm) above top of pan, turn oven up to 400°F (200°C).

14. From time of turning heat up, bake 30 to 45 min or till sides and bottom are nicely browned.

Yogurt or Sour Cream Bread / This bread has a fine texture and a delectable tang. It's wonderful for sandwiches.

3 loaves	1 loaf		1 loaf	3 loaves
1-1/2 Tbsp.	1/2 Tbsp.	sugar	7 mL	21 mL
3 Tbsp.	1 Tbsp.	active dry or fast-rise yeast	15 mL	45 mL
3/4 cup	1/4 cup	cool or lukewarm water	60 mL	180 mL
6 cups	2 cups	all-purpose flour (or equal parts all-purpose and wholewheat flour)	480 mL	1440 mL
1-1/2 cup	1/2 cup	gluten flour	120 mL	360 mL
1-1/2 cup	1/2 cup	wheat germ (or less or omit)	120 mL	360 mL
3 tsp.	1 tsp.	salt or sea salt	5 mL	15 mL
2/3 tsp.	1/3 tsp.	calcium ascorbate powder	2 mL	4 mL
2-1/4 cups	3/4 cup	yogurt or sour cream	180 mL	540 mL
1-1/2 cups	1/2 cup	hot tap water	120 mL	360 mL

1. Measure sugar into wide measuring cup. With same spoon, measure and add yeast.

2. Add cool or lukewarm water. Stir (lumps don't matter). Set in warm, draft-free place till needed (10 to 25 min).

3. Measure dry ingredients into plastic bowl. Mix well.

4. Add yogurt or sour cream and hot tap water to dry ingredients.

5. Immediately add yeast mixture and mix everything together very well with big spoon.

6. If some of the dry mixture won't mix in fairly easily, add a *little* more hot tap water.

7. Lay food wrap right over dough, touching surface. Cover bowl loosely. Set in warm, draft-free place.

8. After 30 min, dough should be about double in bulk. Peel off food wrap. Turn dough out on generously floured cookie sheet or board.

9. With generously floured hands, form loaf (or loaves).

10. Brush off extra flour. Spray bottom and sides of loaf with water.

11. Oil loaf pan. Set loaf in pan and spray top with water.

12. Set bread into oven and turn oven to its *lowest* setting. Leave 10 to 25 min.

13. When dough has risen 1 to 2 in. (2.5 to 5.0 cm) above top of pan, turn oven up to 400°F (200°C).

14. From time of turning heat up, bake 30 to 45 min or till sides and bottom are nicely browned.

We ate this bread — the entire loaf — at an outdoor production of A Midsummer Night's Dream, *with a few fresh tomatoes sliced on top. It was all very European and delicious. We were the envy of everyone around us.*
— *Taster Lynn Patterson*

Tea Bread / *Many dried fruits are suitable in this unique bread. Try matching the fruit to the tea flavor; for example, use dried currants with black-currant tea.*

3 loaves	1 loaf		1 loaf	3 loaves
1-1/2 Tbsp.	1/2 Tbsp.	sugar	7 mL	21 mL
3 Tbsp.	1 Tbsp.	active dry or fast-rise yeast	15 mL	45 mL
3/4 cup	1/4 cup	cool or lukewarm water	60 mL	180 mL
6 cups	2 cups	all-purpose flour (or equal parts all-purpose and wholewheat flour)	480 mL	1440 mL
1-1/2 cup	1/2 cup	gluten flour	120 mL	360 mL
1-1/2 cup	1/2 cup	wheat germ (or less or omit)	120 mL	360 mL
1-1/2 cup	1/2 cup	milk powder	120 mL	360 mL
3 tsp.	1 tsp.	salt or sea salt	5 mL	15 mL
2/3 tsp.	1/3 tsp.	calcium ascorbate powder	2 mL	4 mL
1 cup	1/3 cup	brown or white sugar (or less or omit)	80 mL	240 mL
3 Tbsp.	1 Tbsp.	cinnamon	15 mL	45 mL
3/4 tsp.	1/4 tsp.	nutmeg	1.5 mL	4.5 mL
2-1/4 cups	3/4 cup	dried fruit, e.g., currants, raisins, dried apricots, apples, peaches, pears, cherries	180 mL	540 mL
3/4 cup	1/4 cup	soft shortening or oil (or less or omit)	60 mL	180 mL
3 cups	1 cup	strong tea at temperature of hot tap water	240 mL	720 mL

1. If fruit is very dry, soak it for a few minutes. If pieces are large, chop to size of large raisins.

2. Measure sugar into wide measuring cup. With same spoon, measure and add yeast.

3. Add cool or lukewarm water. Stir (lumps don't matter). Set in warm, draft-free place till needed (10 to 25 min).

4. Measure dry ingredients into plastic bowl. Mix well.

5. Add shortening to dry ingredients, and then the tea at the temperature of hot tap water.

6. Immediately add yeast mixture and mix everything together very well with big spoon.

7. If some of the dry mixture won't mix in fairly easily, add a *little* more hot tap water.

8. Lay food wrap right over dough, touching surface. Cover bowl loosely. Set in warm, draft-free place.

9. After 30 min, dough should be about double in bulk. Peel off food wrap. Turn dough out on generously floured cookie sheet or board.

10. With generously floured hands, form loaf (or loaves).

11. Brush off extra flour. Spray bottom and sides of loaf with water.

12. Oil loaf pan. Set loaf in pan and spray top with water.

13. If desired, sprinkle cinnamon on top.

14. Set bread into oven and turn oven to its *lowest* setting. Leave 10 to 25 min.

15. When dough has risen 1 to 2 in. (2.5 to 5.0 cm) above top of pan, turn oven up to 400°F (200°C).

16. From time of turning heat up, bake 30 to 45 min or till sides and bottom are nicely browned.

Orange Bread / *The orange flavor in this bread has the happy ability to stand on its own, or to harmonize with toppings such as cottage cheese, cream cheese, jam, or marmalade.*

3 loaves	1 loaf		1 loaf	3 loaves
1-1/2 Tbsp.	1/2 Tbsp.	sugar	7 mL	21 mL
3 Tbsp.	1 Tbsp.	active dry or fast-rise yeast	15 mL	45 mL
3/4 cup	1/4 cup	cool or lukewarm water	60 mL	180 mL
6 cups	2 cups	all-purpose flour (or equal parts all-purpose and wholewheat flour)	480 mL	1440 mL
1-1/2 cup	1/2 cup	gluten flour	120 mL	360 mL
1-1/2 cup	1/2 cup	milk powder	120 mL	360 mL
3 tsp.	1 tsp.	salt or sea salt	5 mL	15 mL
2/3 tsp.	1/3 tsp.	calcium ascorbate powder	2 mL	4 mL
1 cup	1/3 cup	brown or white sugar (or less or omit)	80 mL	240 mL
3 Tbsp.	1 Tbsp.	cinnamon	15 mL	45 mL
3 Tbsp.	1 Tbsp.	grated orange rind	15 mL	45 mL
3/4 cup	1/4 cup	soft margarine or butter (or less or omit)	60 mL	180 mL
3 cups	1 cup	orange juice at temperature of hot tap water	240 mL	720 mL

1. Measure sugar into wide measuring cup. With same spoon, measure and add yeast.

2. Add cool or lukewarm water. Stir (lumps don't matter). Set in warm, draft-free place till needed (10 to 25 min).

3. Measure dry ingredients into plastic bowl. Mix well.

4. Add shortening to dry ingredients, and then orange juice at temperature of hot tap water.

5. Immediately add yeast mixture and mix everything together very well with big spoon.

6. If some of the dry mixture won't mix in fairly easily, add a *little* more hot tap water.

7. Lay food wrap right over dough, touching surface. Cover bowl loosely. Set in warm, draft-free place.

8. After 30 min, dough should be about double in bulk. Peel off food wrap. Turn dough out on generously floured cookie sheet or board.

9. With generously floured hands, form loaf (or loaves).

10. Brush off extra flour. Spray bottom and sides of loaf with water.

11. Oil loaf pan. Set loaf in pan and spray top with water.

12. If desired, sprinkle cinnamon on top.

13. Set bread into oven and turn oven to its *lowest* setting. Leave 10 to 25 min.

14. When dough has risen 1 to 2 in. (2.5 to 5.0 cm) above top of pan, turn oven up to 400°F (200°C).

15. From time of turning heat up, bake 30 to 45 min or till sides and bottom are nicely browned.

I truly think this bread is going to be an inspiration to me. Who knows? Maybe even I will learn how to make it.
— Taster Sherry Kornblum

Cottage Cheese Herb Bread / *Chopped fresh dill and chives make this bread particularly delicious. Or if you wish, experiment with another herb combination.*

3 loaves	1 loaf		1 loaf	3 loaves
1-1/2 Tbsp.	1/2 Tbsp.	sugar	7 mL	21 mL
3 Tbsp.	1 Tbsp.	active dry or fast-rise yeast	15 mL	45 mL
3/4 cup	1/4 cup	cool or lukewarm water	60 mL	180 mL
6 cups	2 cups	all-purpose flour (or equal parts all-purpose and wholewheat flour)	480 mL	1440 mL
1-1/2 cup	1/2 cup	gluten flour	120 mL	360 mL
3/4 cup	1/4 cup	wheat germ (or less or omit)	60 mL	180 mL
3 tsp.	1 tsp.	salt or sea salt	5 mL	15 mL
2/3 tsp.	1/3 tsp.	calcium ascorbate powder	2 mL	4 mL
6 Tbsp.	2 Tbsp.	chopped fresh herbs, e.g., dill, chives, thyme, parsley, rosemary, sage, tarragon	30 mL	90 mL
3 Tbsp.	1 Tbsp.	soft shortening or oil (or less or omit)	15 mL	45 mL
3 cups	1 cup	small curd cottage cheese	240 mL	720 mL
3	1	egg(s), slightly beaten	1	3
1-1/2 cup	1/2 cup	hot tap water	120 mL	360 mL

1. Measure sugar into wide measuring cup. With same spoon, measure and add yeast.

2. Add cool or lukewarm water. Stir (lumps don't matter). Set in warm, draft-free place till needed (10 to 25 min).

3. Measure dry ingredients and herbs into plastic bowl. Mix well.

4. Add shortening, cottage cheese, slightly beaten egg(s), and hot tap water to dry ingredients.

5. Immediately add yeast mixture and mix everything together very well with big spoon.

6. If some of the dry mixture won't mix in fairly easily, add a *little* more hot tap water.

7. Lay food wrap right over dough, touching surface. Cover bowl loosely. Set in warm, draft-free place.

8. After 30 min, dough should be about double in bulk. Peel off food wrap. Turn dough out on generously floured cookie sheet or board.

9. With generously floured hands, form loaf (or loaves).

10. Brush off extra flour. Spray bottom and sides of loaf with water.

11. Oil loaf pan. Set loaf in pan and spray top with water.

12. Set bread into oven and turn oven to its *lowest* setting. Leave 10 to 25 min.

13. When dough has risen 1 to 2 in. (2.5 to 5.0 cm) above top of pan, turn oven up to 400°F (200°C).

14. From time of turning heat up, bake 30 to 45 min or till sides and bottom are nicely browned.

WHITE OR BROWN BREADS 45

Raisin Bread / *This is a favorite for breakfast at our house. It's especially good toasted.*

3 loaves	1 loaf		1 loaf	3 loaves
1-1/2 Tbsp.	1/2 Tbsp.	sugar	7 mL	21 mL
3 Tbsp.	1 Tbsp.	active dry or fast-rise yeast	15 mL	45 mL
3/4 cup	1/4 cup	cool or lukewarm water	60 mL	180 mL
6 cups	2 cups	all-purpose flour (or equal parts all-purpose and wholewheat flour)	480 mL	1440 mL
1-1/2 cup	1/2 cup	gluten flour	120 mL	360 mL
1-1/2 cup	1/2 cup	milk powder	120 mL	360 mL
3 tsp.	1 tsp.	salt or sea salt	5 mL	15 mL
2/3 tsp.	1/3 tsp.	calcium ascorbate powder	2 mL	4 mL
1 cup	1/3 cup	brown or white sugar (or less or omit)	80 mL	240 mL
2-1/4 cups	3/4 cup	raisins (soak a few minutes if they're hard)	180 mL	540 mL
1-1/2 cup	1/2 cup	soft margarine or butter (or less)	120 mL	360 mL
6	2	eggs, slightly beaten	2	6
1-1/2 cup	1/2 cup	hot tap water	120 mL	360 mL

1. Measure sugar into wide measuring cup. With same spoon, measure and add yeast.

2. Add cool or lukewarm water. Stir (lumps don't matter). Set in warm, draft-free place till needed (10 to 25 min).

3. Measure dry ingredients into plastic bowl. Mix well.

4. Add margarine or butter, slightly beaten eggs, and hot tap water to dry ingredients.

5. Immediately add yeast mixture and mix everything together very well with big spoon.

6. If some of the dry mixture won't mix in fairly easily, add a *little* more hot tap water.

7. Lay food wrap right over dough, touching surface. Cover bowl loosely. Set in warm, draft-free place.

8. After 30 min, dough should be about double in bulk. Peel off food wrap. Turn dough out on generously floured cookie sheet or board.

9. With generously floured hands, form loaf (or loaves).

10. Brush off extra flour. Spray bottom and sides of loaf with water.

11. Oil loaf pan. Set loaf in pan and spray top with water.

12. Set bread into oven and turn oven to its *lowest* setting. Leave 10 to 25 min.

13. When dough has risen 1 to 2 in. (2.5 to 5.0 cm) above top of pan, turn oven up to 375°F (190°C).

14. From time of turning heat up, bake 40 to 50 min or till sides and bottom are nicely browned.

Spanish Cornbread / *This firm-textured bread has the distinctive flavor that only cornmeal can provide. It's best eaten fresh. Like all BREADSPEED breads, Spanish cornbread freezes beautifully.*

3 loaves	1 loaf		1 loaf	3 loaves
1-1/2 Tbsp.	1/2 Tbsp.	sugar	7 mL	21 mL
3 Tbsp.	1 Tbsp.	active dry or fast-rise yeast	15 mL	45 mL
3/4 cup	1/4 cup	cool or lukewarm water	60 mL	180 mL
6 cups	2 cups	all-purpose flour (or equal parts all-purpose and wholewheat flour)	480 mL	1440 mL
1-1/2 cup	1/2 cup	gluten flour	120 mL	360 mL
3/8 cup	1/8 cup	soy flour (or less or omit)	30 mL	90 mL
3 cups	1 cup	yellow or white cornmeal	240 mL	720 mL
1-1/2 cup	1/2 cup	milk powder	120 mL	360 mL
3 tsp.	1 tsp.	salt or sea salt	5 mL	15 mL
2/3 tsp.	1/3 tsp.	calcium ascorbate powder	2 mL	4 mL
3/8 cup	1/8 cup	soft shortening or oil (or less or more)	30 mL	90 mL
3-3/4 cups	1-1/4 cup	hot tap water	300 mL	900 mL

1. Measure sugar into wide measuring cup. With same spoon, measure and add yeast.

2. Add cool or lukewarm water. Stir (lumps don't matter). Set in warm, draft-free place till needed (10 to 25 min).

3. Measure dry ingredients into plastic bowl. Mix well.

4. Add shortening and hot tap water to dry ingredients.

5. Immediately add yeast mixture and mix everything together very well with big spoon.

6. If some of the dry mixture won't mix in fairly easily, add a *little* more hot tap water.

7. Lay food wrap right over dough, touching surface. Cover bowl loosely. Set in warm, draft-free place.

8. After 30 min, dough should be about double in bulk. Peel off food wrap. Turn dough out on generously floured cookie sheet or board.

9. With generously floured hands, form round loaf (or loaves) about 7 in. (17 cm) across. Brush off extra flour.

10. Oil a cookie sheet. Set loaf on cookie sheet and spray with water. With a sharp knife, cut a cross on the top. Sprinkle top generously with cornmeal.

11. Set bread into oven and turn oven to its *lowest* setting. Leave 10 to 25 min.

12. When loaf has about doubled in size, turn oven up to 400°F (200°C).

13. From time of turning heat up, bake 30 to 45 min or till sides and bottom are nicely browned.

Finnish Emergency Bread / You can bake this bread when facing an emergency (Finnish or otherwise) requiring you to have hot yeast bread on the table in an hour. It looks interesting and tastes great.

3 loaves	1 loaf		1 loaf	3 loaves
1-1/2 Tbsp.	1/2 Tbsp.	sugar	7 mL	21 mL
3 Tbsp.	1 Tbsp.	active dry or fast-rise yeast	15 mL	45 mL
3/4 cup	1/4 cup	cool or lukewarm water	60 mL	180 mL
4-1/2 cups	1-1/2 cups	all-purpose flour (or substitute rye flour for 1/3 of specified amount)	360 mL	1080 mL
1-1/2 cup	1/2 cup	gluten flour	120 mL	360 mL
1-1/2 cup	1/2 cup	wheat germ (or less or omit)	120 mL	360 mL
1-1/2 cup	1/2 cup	milk powder	120 mL	360 mL
3 tsp.	1 tsp.	salt or sea salt	5 mL	15 mL
2/3 tsp.	1/3 tsp.	calcium ascorbate powder	2 mL	4 mL
3/8 cup	1/8 cup	soft shortening or oil (or less or more)	30 mL	90 mL
3/8 cup	1/8 cup	molasses (omit if not using rye flour)	30 mL	90 mL
2-1/4 cups	3/4 cup	hot tap water	180 mL	540 mL

1. Measure sugar into wide measuring cup. With same spoon, measure and add yeast.

2. Add cool or lukewarm water. Stir (lumps don't matter). Set in warm, draft-free place till needed (10 to 25 min).

3. Measure dry ingredients into plastic bowl. Mix well.

4. Add shortening, molasses, and hot tap water to dry ingredients.

5. Immediately add yeast mixture and mix everything together very well with big spoon.

6. If some of the dry mixture won't mix in fairly easily, add a *little* more hot tap water.

7. Turn dough out on generously floured cookie sheet or board.

8. With generously floured hands, form round loaf (or loaves) about 8 in. (20 cm) across. Brush off extra flour.

9. Oil a cookie sheet. Set loaf on cookie sheet and spray with water.

10. Set bread into oven and turn oven to its *lowest* setting. Leave 10 to 20 min.

11. When loaf has about doubled in size, turn oven up to 375°F (190°C).

12. From time of turning heat up, bake 15 to 20 min or till nicely browned. Watch the bottom, as it can burn if bread is baked too long.

"A loaf of bread," the Walrus said,
"Is what we chiefly need."
— Lewis Carroll

Standard Wholewheat Bread / This is worth baking for the aroma alone. But don't stop with the aroma.

3 loaves	1 loaf		1 loaf	3 loaves
1-1/2 Tbsp.	1/2 Tbsp.	brown sugar	7 mL	21 mL
3 Tbsp.	1 Tbsp.	active dry or fast-rise yeast	15 mL	45 mL
3/4 cup	1/4 cup	cool or lukewarm water	60 mL	180 mL
3 cups	1 cup	all-purpose flour	240 mL	720 mL
3 cups	1 cup	wholewheat flour	240 mL	720 mL
1-1/2 cup	1/2 cup	gluten flour	120 mL	360 mL
1-1/2 cup	1/2 cup	wheat germ (or less or omit)	120 mL	360 mL
1-1/2 cup	1/2 cup	cracked wheat (or less or omit)	120 mL	360 mL
1-1/2 cup	1/2 cup	milk powder	120 mL	360 mL
3 tsp.	1 tsp.	salt or sea salt	5 mL	15 mL
2/3 tsp.	1/3 tsp.	calcium ascorbate powder	2 mL	4 mL
3/8 cup	1/8 cup	soft shortening or oil (or less or more)	30 mL	90 mL
3/4 cup	1/4 cup	molasses or honey (or less or omit)	60 mL	180 mL
3 cups	1 cup	hot tap water	240 mL	720 mL

1. Measure brown sugar into wide measuring cup. With same spoon, measure and add yeast.

2. Add cool or lukewarm water. Stir (lumps don't matter). Set in warm, draft-free place till needed (10 to 25 min).

3. Measure dry ingredients into plastic bowl. Mix well.

4. Add shortening, molasses or honey, and hot tap water to dry ingredients.

5. Immediately add yeast mixture and mix everything together very well with big spoon.

6. If some of the dry mixture won't mix in fairly easily, add a *little* more hot tap water.

7. Lay food wrap right over dough, touching surface. Cover bowl loosely. Set in warm, draft-free place.

8. After 30 min, dough should be about double in bulk. Peel off food wrap. Turn dough out on generously floured cookie sheet or board.

9. With generously floured hands, form loaf (or loaves).

10. Brush off extra flour. Spray bottom and sides of loaf with water.

11. Oil loaf pan. Set loaf in pan and spray top with water.

12. If desired, sprinkle cracked wheat on top.

13. Set bread into oven and turn oven to its *lowest* setting. Leave 10 to 25 min.

14. When dough has risen 1 to 2 in. (2.5 to 5.0 cm) above top of pan, turn oven up to 400°F (200°C).

15. From time of turning heat up, bake 30 to 45 min or till sides and bottom are nicely browned.

What impresses me most is this bread's texture and moistness. Your bread gives new meaning to wholewheat bread. I can't rave enough about how much I like it.
— Taster Sharon Ord Delisle

Granola Bread / *How's this for streamlining breakfast? You can have your cereal and toast all in one.*

3 loaves	1 loaf		1 loaf	3 loaves
1-1/2 Tbsp.	1/2 Tbsp.	brown sugar	7 mL	21 mL
3 Tbsp.	1 Tbsp.	active dry or fast-rise yeast	15 mL	45 mL
3/4 cup	1/4 cup	cool or lukewarm water	60 mL	180 mL
3 cups	1 cup	all-purpose flour	240 mL	720 mL
3 cups	1 cup	wholewheat flour	240 mL	720 mL
1-1/2 cup	1/2 cup	gluten flour	120 mL	360 mL
3 cups	1 cup	granola	240 mL	720 mL
1-1/2 cup	1/2 cup	milk powder	120 mL	360 mL
3 tsp.	1 tsp.	salt or sea salt	5 mL	15 mL
2/3 tsp.	1/3 tsp.	calcium ascorbate powder	2 mL	4 mL
3 Tbsp.	1 Tbsp.	cinnamon	15 mL	45 mL
3/4 tsp.	1/4 tsp.	nutmeg	1.5 mL	4.5 mL
1-1/2 cup	1/2 cup	raisins (soak a few minutes if they're hard)	120 mL	360 mL
3/8 cup	1/8 cup	soft shortening or oil (or less or more)	30 mL	90 mL
3/4 cup	1/4 cup	molasses or honey (or less or omit)	60 mL	180 mL
3 cups	1 cup	hot tap water	240 mL	720 mL

1. Measure brown sugar into wide measuring cup. With same spoon, measure and add yeast.

2. Add cool or lukewarm water. Stir (lumps don't matter). Set in warm, draft-free place till needed (10 to 25 min).

3. Measure dry ingredients into plastic bowl. Mix well.

4. Add shortening, molasses or honey, and hot tap water to dry ingredients.

5. Immediately add yeast mixture and mix everything together very well with big spoon.

6. If some of the dry mixture won't mix in fairly easily, add a *little* more hot tap water.

7. Lay food wrap right over dough, touching surface. Cover bowl loosely. Set in warm, draft-free place.

8. After 30 min, dough should be about double in bulk. Peel off food wrap. Turn dough out on generously floured cookie sheet or board.

9. With generously floured hands, form loaf (or loaves).

10. Brush off extra flour. Spray bottom and sides of loaf with water.

11. Oil loaf pan. Set loaf in pan and spray top with water.

12. If desired, sprinkle wholewheat flour or sesame seeds on top.

13. Set bread into oven and turn oven to its *lowest* setting. Leave 10 to 25 min.

14. When dough has risen 1 to 2 in. (2.5 to 5.0 cm) above top of pan, turn oven up to 400°F (200°C).

15. From time of turning heat up, bake 30 to 45 min or till sides and bottom are nicely browned.

MOR Rye Bread / *I call this MOR because it's "middle of the road" rye bread — not really dark and not really light. Also it's MOR bread because, after you eat one slice, you want more!*

3 loaves	1 loaf		1 loaf	3 loaves
1-1/2 Tbsp.	1/2 Tbsp.	brown sugar	7 mL	21 mL
3 Tbsp.	1 Tbsp.	active dry or fast-rise yeast	15 mL	45 mL
3/4 cup	1/4 cup	cool or lukewarm water	60 mL	180 mL
3 cups	1 cup	all-purpose flour	240 mL	720 mL
3 cups	1 cup	wholewheat flour	240 mL	720 mL
1-1/2 cup	1/2 cup	gluten flour	120 mL	360 mL
3 cups	1 cup	rye flour	240 mL	720 mL
3/4 cup	1/4 cup	sunflower seeds (or less or more)	60 mL	180 mL
1-1/2 cup	1/2 cup	milk powder	120 mL	360 mL
3 tsp.	1 tsp.	salt or sea salt	5 mL	15 mL
2/3 tsp.	1/3 tsp.	calcium ascorbate powder	2 mL	4 mL
3/8 cup	1/8 cup	soft shortening or oil (or less or more)	30 mL	90 mL
3/4 cup	1/4 cup	molasses or honey (or less or omit)	60 mL	180 mL
3 cups	1 cup	hot tap water	240 mL	720 mL

1. Measure brown sugar into wide measuring cup. With same spoon, measure and add yeast.

2. Add cool or lukewarm water. Stir (lumps don't matter). Set in warm, draft-free place till needed (10 to 25 min).

3. Measure dry ingredients into plastic bowl. Mix well.

4. Add shortening, molasses or honey, and hot tap water to dry ingredients.

5. Immediately add yeast mixture and mix everything together very well with big spoon.

6. If some of the dry mixture won't mix in fairly easily, add a *little* more hot tap water.

7. Lay food wrap right over dough, touching surface. Cover bowl loosely. Set in warm, draft-free place.

8. After 30 min, dough should be about double in bulk. Peel off food wrap. Turn dough out on generously floured cookie sheet or board.

9. With generously floured hands, form loaf (or loaves).

10. Brush off extra flour. Spray bottom and sides of loaf with water.

11. Oil loaf pan. Set loaf in pan and spray top with water.

12. If desired, sprinkle rye flour on top.

13. Set bread into oven and turn oven to its *lowest* setting. Leave 10 to 25 min.

14. When dough has risen 1 to 2 in. (2.5 to 5.0 cm) above top of pan, turn oven up to 400°F (200°C).

15. From time of turning heat up, bake 30 to 45 min or till sides and bottom are nicely browned.

If you have two loaves of bread, sell one and buy a hyacinth.
— Persian proverb

Bob's Oatmeal Bread / *This is one of my husband's favorites. It's a great bread to take to a community supper, picnic, or barbecue.*

3 loaves	1 loaf		1 loaf	3 loaves
1-1/2 Tbsp.	1/2 Tbsp.	sugar	7 mL	21 mL
3 Tbsp.	1 Tbsp.	active dry or fast-rise yeast	15 mL	45 mL
3/4 cup	1/4 cup	cool or lukewarm water	60 mL	180 mL
3 cups	1 cup	all-purpose flour	240 mL	720 mL
3 cups	1 cup	wholewheat flour	240 mL	720 mL
3 cups	1 cup	quick-cooking oatmeal (uncooked)	240 mL	720 mL
1-1/2 cup	1/2 cup	gluten flour	120 mL	360 mL
1-1/2 cup	1/2 cup	wheat germ (or less or omit)	120 mL	360 mL
1-1/2 cup	1/2 cup	milk powder	120 mL	360 mL
3 tsp.	1 tsp.	salt or sea salt	5 mL	15 mL
2/3 tsp.	1/3 tsp.	calcium ascorbate powder	2 mL	4 mL
3/4 cup	1/4 cup	brown sugar (or less or omit)	60 mL	180 mL
3/8 cup	1/8 cup	soft shortening or oil (or less or more)	30 mL	90 mL
3 cups	1 cup	hot tap water	240 mL	720 mL

1. Measure sugar into wide measuring cup. With same spoon, measure and add yeast.

2. Add cool or lukewarm water. Stir (lumps don't matter). Set in warm, draft-free place till needed (10 to 25 min).

3. Measure dry ingredients into plastic bowl. Mix well.

4. Add shortening and hot tap water to dry ingredients.

5. Immediately add yeast mixture and mix everything together very well with big spoon.

6. If some of the dry mixture won't mix in fairly easily, add a *little* more hot tap water.

7. Lay food wrap right over dough, touching surface. Cover bowl loosely. Set in warm, draft-free place.

8. After 30 min, dough should be about double in bulk. Peel off food wrap. Turn dough out on generously floured cookie sheet or board.

9. With generously floured hands, form loaf (or loaves).

10. Brush off extra flour. Spray bottom and sides of loaf with water.

11. Oil loaf pan. Set loaf in pan and spray top with water.

12. If desired, sprinkle oatmeal on top.

13. Set bread into oven and turn oven to its *lowest* setting. Leave 10 to 25 min.

14. When dough has risen 1 to 2 in. (2.5 to 5.0 cm) above top of pan, turn oven up to 400°F (200°C).

15. From time of turning heat up, bake 30 to 45 min or till sides and bottom are nicely browned.

Peanut Butter Bread / *"This is a fun bread,"* says one taster. *"It is very wholesome,"* says another taster, *"and at the same time particularly yummy!"*

3 loaves	1 loaf		1 loaf	3 loaves
1-1/2 Tbsp.	1/2 Tbsp.	brown sugar	7 mL	21 mL
3 Tbsp.	1 Tbsp.	active dry or fast-rise yeast	15 mL	45 mL
3/4 cup	1/4 cup	cool or lukewarm water	60 mL	180 mL
3 cups	1 cup	all-purpose flour	240 mL	720 mL
3 cups	1 cup	wholewheat flour	240 mL	720 mL
1-1/2 cup	1/2 cup	gluten flour	120 mL	360 mL
1-1/2 cup	1/2 cup	milk powder	120 mL	360 mL
3 tsp.	1 tsp.	salt or sea salt	5 mL	15 mL
2/3 tsp.	1/3 tsp.	calcium ascorbate powder	2 mL	4 mL
1-1/2 cup	1/2 cup	chopped peanuts (or less or omit)	120 mL	720 mL
2 cups	2/3 cup	peanut butter	160 mL	480 mL
3/4 cup	1/4 cup	molasses or honey (or less or omit)	60 mL	180 mL
2 cups	2/3 cup	hot tap water	160 mL	480 mL

1. Measure brown sugar into wide measuring cup. With same spoon, measure and add yeast.

2. Add cool or lukewarm water. Stir (lumps don't matter). Set in warm, draft-free place till needed (10 to 25 min).

3. Measure dry ingredients into plastic bowl. Mix well.

4. Add peanut butter, molasses or honey, and hot tap water to dry ingredients.

5. Immediately add yeast mixture and mix everything together very well with big spoon.

6. If some of the dry mixture won't mix in fairly easily, add a *little* more hot tap water.

7. Lay food wrap right over dough, touching surface. Cover bowl loosely. Set in warm, draft-free place.

8. After 30 min, dough should be about double in bulk. Peel off food wrap. Turn dough out on generously floured cookie sheet or board.

9. With generously floured hands, form loaf (or loaves).

10. Brush off extra flour. Spray bottom and sides of loaf with water.

11. Oil loaf pan. Set loaf in pan and spray top with water.

12. If desired, sprinkle cracked wheat on top.

13. Set bread into oven and turn oven to its *lowest* setting. Leave 10 to 25 min.

14. When dough has risen 1 to 2 in. (2.5 to 5.0 cm) above top of pan, turn oven up to 400°F (200°C).

15. From time of turning heat up, bake 30 to 45 min or till sides and bottom are nicely browned.

Comfort thine heart with a morsel of bread.
— The Bible, Judges 19:5

Jammy Bread / You can use this wholesome bread to reward the kids for getting into their "jammies," ready for bed. It makes a great bedtime snack for grownups, too!

3 loaves	1 loaf		1 loaf	3 loaves
1-1/2 Tbsp.	1/2 Tbsp.	sugar	7 mL	21 mL
3 Tbsp.	1 Tbsp.	active dry or fast-rise yeast	15 mL	45 mL
3/4 cup	1/4 cup	cool or lukewarm water	60 mL	180 mL
3 cups	1 cup	all-purpose flour	240 mL	720 mL
3 cups	1 cup	wholewheat flour	240 mL	720 mL
1-1/2 cup	1/2 cup	gluten flour	120 mL	360 mL
1-1/2 cup	1/2 cup	wheat germ (or less or omit)	120 mL	360 mL
1-1/2 cup	1/2 cup	cracked wheat (or less or omit)	120 mL	360 mL
1-1/2 cup	1/2 cup	milk powder	120 mL	360 mL
3 tsp.	1 tsp.	salt or sea salt	5 mL	15 mL
2/3 tsp.	1/3 tsp.	calcium ascorbate powder	2 mL	4 mL
3 tsp.	1 tsp.	ground cloves	5 mL	15 mL
1-1/2 tsp.	1/2 tsp.	ground nutmeg	2.5 mL	7.5 mL
3/8 cup	1/8 cup	soft shortening or oil (or less or more)	30 mL	90 mL
3 cups	1 cup	hot tap water	240 mL	720 mL
3 cups	1 cup	jam or marmalade	240 mL	720 mL

1. Measure sugar into wide measuring cup. With same spoon, measure and add yeast.

2. Add cool or lukewarm water. Stir (lumps don't matter). Set in warm, draft-free place till needed (10 to 25 min).

3. Measure dry ingredients into plastic bowl. Mix well.

4. Add shortening and hot tap water to dry ingredients.

5. Immediately add yeast mixture and mix everything together very well with big spoon.

6. If some of the dry mixture won't mix in fairly easily, add a *little* more hot tap water.

7. Lay food wrap right over dough, touching surface. Cover bowl loosely. Set in warm, draft-free place.

8. After 30 min, dough should be about double in bulk. Peel off food wrap. Turn dough out on generously floured cookie sheet or board.

9. With generously floured hands, pat dough (for each loaf) into a rectangle about 10 in. by 16 in. (25 cm by 40 cm). Spread jam on the rectangle, stopping about 2 in. (5 cm) short of the edges. Roll up like a jelly roll, turn ends under, and seal seams to form a loaf (or loaves).

10. Brush off extra flour. Spray bottom and sides of loaf with water.

11. Oil loaf pan. Set loaf in pan and spray top with water.

12. If desired, sprinkle nutmeg on top.

13. Set bread into oven and turn oven to its *lowest* setting. Leave 10 to 25 min.

14. When dough has risen 1 to 2 in. (2.5 to 5.0 cm) above top of pan, turn oven up to 375°F (190°C).

15. From time of turning heat up, bake 40 to 50 min or till sides and bottom are nicely browned. Some of the jam may bubble out during baking, but this doesn't usually cause a problem. If you think it may bubble over, set a pan underneath to catch any drips.

Mom's Wholewheat Bread / This is an adaptation of the bread I enjoyed so much as a child. Hearty, wheaty, and satisfying, it could easily become one of your all-time favorites, too.

3 loaves	1 loaf		1 loaf	3 loaves
1-1/2 Tbsp.	1/2 Tbsp.	brown sugar	7 mL	21 mL
3 Tbsp.	1 Tbsp.	active dry or fast-rise yeast	15 mL	45 mL
3/4 cup	1/4 cup	cool or lukewarm water	60 mL	180 mL
6 cups	2 cups	wholewheat flour	480 mL	1440 mL
1-1/2 cup	1/2 cup	gluten flour	120 mL	360 mL
1-1/2 cup	1/2 cup	cracked wheat (or less or omit)	120 mL	360 mL
1-1/2 cup	1/2 cup	milk powder	120 mL	360 mL
3 tsp.	1 tsp.	salt or sea salt	5 mL	15 mL
2/3 tsp.	1/3 tsp.	calcium ascorbate powder	2 mL	4 mL
3/8 cup	1/8 cup	soft shortening or oil (or less or more)	30 mL	90 mL
3/4 cup	1/4 cup	molasses or honey (or less or omit)	60 mL	180 mL
3 cups	1 cup	hot tap water	240 mL	720 mL

1. Measure brown sugar into wide measuring cup. With same spoon, measure and add yeast.

2. Add cool or lukewarm water. Stir (lumps don't matter). Set in warm, draft-free place till needed (10 to 25 min).

3. Measure dry ingredients into plastic bowl. Mix well.

4. Add shortening, molasses or honey, and hot tap water to dry ingredients.

5. Immediately add yeast mixture and mix everything together very well with big spoon.

6. If some of the dry mixture won't mix in fairly easily, add a *little* more hot tap water.

7. Lay food wrap right over dough, touching surface. Cover bowl loosely. Set in warm, draft-free place.

8. After 30 min, dough should be about double in bulk. Peel off food wrap. Turn dough out on generously floured cookie sheet or board.

9. With generously floured hands, form loaf (or loaves).

10. Brush off extra flour. Spray bottom and sides of loaf with water.

11. Oil loaf pan. Set loaf in pan and spray top with water.

12. If desired, sprinkle cracked wheat or wholewheat flour on top.

13. Set bread into oven and turn oven to its *lowest* setting. Leave 10 to 25 min.

14. When dough has risen 1 to 2 in. (2.5 to 5.0 cm) above top of pan, turn oven up to 400°F (200°C).

15. From time of turning heat up, bake 30 to 45 min or till sides and bottom are nicely browned.

This bread smells good and tastes excellent. I rate the crust 100% plus.
— Taster George Christoffer

Black Russian / *This bread is wonderful with cheese, cream cheese, marmalade, honey, or molasses.*

3 loaves	1 loaf		1 loaf	3 loaves
1-1/2 Tbsp.	1/2 Tbsp.	brown sugar	7 mL	21 mL
3 Tbsp.	1 Tbsp.	active dry or fast-rise yeast	15 mL	45 mL
3/4 cup	1/4 cup	cool or lukewarm water	60 mL	180 mL
3-3/4 cups	1-1/4 cup	all-purpose flour	300 mL	900 mL
2-1/4 cups	3/4 cups	rye flour	180 mL	540 mL
1-1/2 cup	1/2 cup	gluten flour	120 mL	360 mL
1-1/2 cup	1/2 cup	wheat germ (or less or omit)	120 mL	360 mL
1-1/2 cup	1/2 cup	cracked wheat (or less or omit)	120 mL	360 mL
3 Tbsp.	1 Tbsp.	caraway seed (or less or omit)	15 mL	45 mL
3/4 cup	1/4 cup	carob powder or cocoa (more or less to taste)	60 mL	180 mL
1-1/2 cup	1/2 cup	milk powder	120 mL	360 mL
3 tsp.	1 tsp.	salt or sea salt	5 mL	15 mL
2/3 tsp.	1/3 tsp.	calcium ascorbate powder	2 mL	4 mL
3/8 cup	1/8 cup	soft shortening or oil (or less or more)	30 mL	90 mL
3/4 cup	1/4 cup	dark molasses	60 mL	180 mL
2 cups	2/3 cup	hot tap water	160 mL	480 mL

1. Measure brown sugar into wide measuring cup. With same spoon, measure and add yeast.

2. Add cool or lukewarm water. Stir (lumps don't matter). Set in warm, draft-free place till needed (10 to 25 min).

3. Measure dry ingredients into plastic bowl. Mix well.

4. Add shortening, molasses, and hot tap water to dry ingredients.

5. Immediately add yeast mixture and mix everything together very well with big spoon.

6. If some of the dry mixture won't mix in fairly easily, add a *little* more hot tap water.

7. Lay food wrap right over dough, touching surface. Cover bowl loosely. Set in warm, draft-free place.

8. After 30 min, dough should be about double in bulk. Peel off food wrap. Turn dough out on generously floured cookie sheet or board.

9. With generously floured hands, form loaf (or loaves).

10. Brush off extra flour. Spray bottom and sides of loaf with water.

11. Oil loaf pan. Set loaf in pan and spray top with water.

12. If desired, sprinkle caraway seed or cracked wheat on top.

13. Set bread into oven and turn oven to its *lowest* setting. Leave 10 to 25 min.

14. When dough has risen 1 to 2 in. (2.5 to 5.0 cm) above top of pan, turn oven up to 400°F (200°C).

15. From time of turning heat up, bake 30 to 45 min or till sides and bottom are nicely browned.

Black and White Russian / *This braided bread produces a dramatic effect when brought whole to the table with a flourish — and a big knife for slicing.*

2 loaves   *2 loaves*

Prepare dough for one loaf of Black Russian bread (see previous two pages). Let it rise while you prepare the following white dough.

1/2 Tbsp.	sugar	7 mL
1 Tbsp.	active dry or fast-rise yeast	15 mL
1/4 cup	cool or lukewarm water	60 mL
2 cups	all-purpose flour	480 mL
1/2 cup	gluten flour	120 mL
1/2 cup	milk powder	120 mL
1 tsp.	salt or sea salt	5 mL
1/3 tsp.	calcium ascorbate powder	2 mL
1/8 cup	soft shortening or oil (or less or more)	30 mL
1 cup	hot tap water	240 mL

1. Measure sugar into wide measuring cup. With same spoon, measure and add yeast.

2. Add cool or lukewarm water. Stir (lumps don't matter). Set in warm, draft-free place till needed (10 to 25 min).

3. Measure dry ingredients into plastic bowl. Mix well.

4. Add shortening and hot tap water to dry ingredients.

5. Immediately add yeast mixture and mix everything together very well with big spoon.

6. If some of the dry mixture won't mix in fairly easily, add a *little* more hot tap water.

7. Lay food wrap right over dough touching surface. Cover bowl loosely. Set in warm, draft-free place.

8. After 30 min, white dough should be about double in bulk. Black Russian dough will probably be more than double, but that's all right. Peel food wrap off both doughs. Turn them out on a generously floured cookie sheet or board.

9. With generously floured hands, roll each dough into a 14-in. (35-cm) length. Braid the two strands, tucking the ends under and sealing them to form 2 loaves (see drawing).

10. Brush off extra flour. Spray bottom and sides of loaf with water.

11. Oil loaf pan. Set loaf in pan and spray top with water.

12. If desired, sprinkle cracked wheat on top.

13. Set bread into oven and turn oven to its *lowest* setting. Leave 10 to 25 min.

14. When dough has risen 1 to 2 in. (2.5 to 5.0 cm) above top of pan, turn oven up to 400°F (200°C).

15. From time of turning heat up, bake 30 to 45 min or till sides and bottom are nicely browned.

BROWN BREADS 69

Cooked Wheat Bread / *How can you make sure you're getting every bit of the nutritional goodness of wheat in your bread? Why not buy the wheat yourself from a bulk food store, health food store, farmer, or mill? Used as directed in this recipe, it makes a wonderfully bouncy and satisfying bread.*

3 loaves	1 loaf		1 loaf	3 loaves
1-1/2 Tbsp.	1/2 Tbsp.	brown sugar	7 mL	21 mL
3 Tbsp.	1 Tbsp.	active dry or fast-rise yeast	15 mL	45 mL
3/4 cup	1/4 cup	cool or lukewarm water	60 mL	180 mL
3 cups	1 cup	all-purpose flour	240 mL	720 mL
3 cups	1 cup	wholewheat flour	240 mL	720 mL
1-1/2 cup	1/2 cup	gluten flour	120 mL	360 mL
1-1/2 cup	1/2 cup	milk powder	120 mL	360 mL
3 tsp.	1 tsp.	salt or sea salt	5 mL	15 mL
2/3 tsp.	1/3 tsp.	calcium ascorbate powder	2 mL	4 mL
2 cups	2/3 cup	clean wheat	160 mL	480 mL
3/8 cup	1/8 cup	soft shortening or oil (or less or more)	30 mL	90 mL
3/4 cup	1/4 cup	molasses or honey (or less or omit)	60 mL	180 mL
2 cups	2/3 cup	hot tap water	160 mL	480 mL

1. Put wheat in saucepan with about twice the amount of water. Cook till wheat is fairly soft — about 20 min.

2. Cool slightly. Then use a blender or food mill to chop the wheat till it's about the consistency of coarse porridge. Drain off any extra water.

3. Measure brown sugar into wide measuring cup. With same spoon, measure and add yeast.

4. Add cool or lukewarm water. Stir (lumps don't matter). Set in warm, draft-free place till needed (10 to 25 min).

5. Measure dry ingredients into plastic bowl. Add prepared wheat and mix well.

6. Add shortening, molasses or honey, and hot tap water to dry ingredients.

7. Immediately add yeast mixture and mix everything together very well with big spoon.

8. If some of the dry mixture won't mix in fairly easily, add a *little* more hot tap water.

9. Lay food wrap right over dough, touching surface. Cover bowl loosely. Set in warm, draft-free place.

10. After 30 min, dough should be about double in bulk. Peel off food wrap. Turn dough out on generously floured cookie sheet or board.

11. With generously floured hands, form loaf (or loaves).

12. Brush off extra flour. Spray bottom and sides of loaf with water.

13. Oil loaf pan. Set loaf in pan and spray top with water.

14. If desired, sprinkle cracked wheat on top.

15. Set bread into oven and turn oven to its *lowest* setting. Leave 10 to 25 min.

16. When dough has risen 1 to 2 in. (2.5 to 5.0 cm) above top of pan, turn oven up to 400°F (200°C).

17. From time of turning heat up, bake 30 to 45 min or till sides and bottom are nicely browned.

Pan Buns / *Since I love brown breads, I prefer these made with wholewheat flour. However, they're good as white buns, too. Made in the size indicated here, they're perfect as an accompaniment to dinner.*

48 buns	16 buns		16 buns	48 buns
1-1/2 Tbsp.	1/2 Tbsp.	sugar	7 mL	21 mL
3 Tbsp.	1 Tbsp.	active dry or fast-rise yeast	15 mL	45 mL
3/4 cup	1/4 cup	cool or lukewarm water	60 mL	180 mL
6 cups	2 cups	all-purpose flour (or for brown buns, use equal parts all-purpose and wholewheat flour)	480 mL	1440 mL
1-1/2 cup	1/2 cup	gluten flour	120 mL	360 mL
1-1/2 cup	1/2 cup	wheat germ (or less or omit)	120 mL	360 mL
3 cups	1 cup	milk powder	240 mL	720 mL
3 tsp.	1 tsp.	salt or sea salt	5 mL	15 mL
2/3 tsp.	1/3 tsp.	calcium ascorbate powder	2 mL	4 mL
1-1/2 cups	1/2 cup	soft shortening or oil	120 mL	360 mL
2-1/4 cups	3/4 cup	hot tap water	180 mL	540 mL

1. Measure sugar into wide measuring cup. With same spoon, measure and add yeast.

2. Add cool or lukewarm water. Stir (lumps don't matter). Set in warm, draft-free place till needed (10 to 25 min).

3. Measure dry ingredients into plastic bowl. Mix well.

4. Add shortening and hot tap water to dry ingredients.

5. Immediately add yeast mixture and mix everything together very well with big spoon.

6. If some of the dry mixture won't mix in fairly easily, add a *little* more hot tap water.

7. Lay food wrap right over dough, touching surface. Cover bowl loosely. Set in warm, draft-free place.

8. After 30 min, dough should be about double in bulk. Peel off food wrap. Turn dough out on generously floured cookie sheet or board.

9. With generously floured hands, form dough into a long, even cylinder (one for each 16 rolls). With a sharp knife, cut the cylinder in half. Cut each of these halves in half, continuing until you have 16 equal-sized chunks of dough.

10. Roll the chunks of dough into balls and set them, just barely touching each other, in an oiled bun pan. Spray with water. If desired, sprinkle with sesame seeds.

11. Set buns into oven and turn oven to its *lowest* setting. Leave 10 to 25 min.

12. When buns have about doubled in size, turn oven up to 400°F (200°C).

13. From time of turning heat up, bake 20 to 25 min or until nicely browned.

Hot Cross Buns / *Bake these for Easter, or for any time of the year. You can make them more or less spicy, according to your taste.*

36 buns	12 buns		12 buns	36 buns
1-1/2 Tbsp.	1/2 Tbsp.	brown sugar	7 mL	21 mL
3 Tbsp.	1 Tbsp.	active dry or fast-rise yeast	15 mL	45 mL
3/4 cup	1/4 cup	cool or lukewarm water	60 mL	180 mL
6 cups	2 cups	all-purpose flour	480 mL	1440 mL
1-1/2 cup	1/2 cup	gluten flour	120 mL	360 mL
1-1/2 cup	1/2 cup	wheat germ (or less or omit)	120 mL	360 mL
1-1/2 cup	1/2 cup	milk powder	120 mL	360 mL
1-1/2 tsp.	1/2 tsp.	salt or sea salt	3 mL	9 mL
2/3 tsp.	1/3 tsp.	calcium ascorbate powder	2 mL	4 mL
3/8 cup	1/8 cup	brown or white sugar	30 mL	90 mL
3-3/4 tsp.	1-1/4 tsp.	cinnamon	6 mL	19 mL
2-1/4 tsp.	3/4 tsp.	allspice	4 mL	11 mL
2-1/4 tsp.	3/4 tsp.	cloves	4 mL	11 mL
2-1/4 cups	3/4 cup	raisins (soak a few minutes if they're hard)	180 mL	540 mL
3/4 cup	1/4 cup	chopped peel (or less or omit)	60 mL	180 mL
3 Tbsp.	1 Tbsp.	soft shortening or oil	15 mL	45 mL
3	1	egg(s), slightly beaten	1	3
2-1/4 cups	3/4 cup	hot tap water	180 mL	540 mL

1. Measure brown sugar into wide measuring cup. With same spoon, measure and add yeast.

2. Add cool or lukewarm water. Stir (lumps don't matter). Set in warm, draft-free place till needed (10 to 25 min).

3. Measure dry ingredients into plastic bowl. Mix well.

4. Add shortening, slightly beaten egg(s), and hot tap water to dry ingredients.

5. Immediately add yeast mixture and mix everything together very well with big spoon.

6. If some of the dry mixture won't mix in fairly easily, add a *little* more hot tap water.

7. Lay food wrap right over dough, touching surface. Cover bowl loosely. Set in warm, draft-free place.

8. After 30 min, dough should be about double in bulk. Peel off food wrap. Turn dough out on generously floured cookie sheet or board.

9. With generously floured hands, form dough into a long, even cylinder (one for each 12 buns). With a sharp knife, cut the cylinder in half. Cut each of these halves in half, and then cut them into thirds so you have 12 equal-sized chunks of dough.

10. Roll the chunks of dough into balls and set them about 1 in. (2.5 cm) apart in an oiled bun pan. Spray with water.

11. Set buns into oven and turn oven to its *lowest* setting. Leave 10 to 25 min.

12. When buns have about doubled in size, turn oven up to 350°F (175°C).

13. From time of turning heat up, bake 20 to 30 min or until nicely browned.

14. Pipe crosses on the tops with icing made by mixing: 8 parts sifted icing sugar, 1 to 2 parts milk, and vanilla extract to taste.

Mom's Paska / *This delicious Easter bread is made by Ukrainians, Mennonites, and other European groups. My mother usually bakes hers as rolls. However, paska may also be baked in oiled pans or coffee tins. If you do this, fill each pan or tin only 1/3 full.*

36 rolls	*12 rolls*		*12 rolls*	*36 rolls*
1-1/2 Tbsp.	1/2 Tbsp.	brown sugar	7 mL	21 mL
3 Tbsp.	1 Tbsp.	active dry or fast-rise yeast	15 mL	45 mL
3/4 cup	1/4 cup	cool or lukewarm water	60 mL	180 mL
6 cups	2 cups	all-purpose flour	480 mL	1440 mL
1-1/2 cup	1/2 cup	gluten flour	120 mL	360 mL
2-1/4 cups	3/4 cup	milk powder	180 mL	540 mL
1-1/2 tsp.	1/2 tsp.	salt or sea salt	3 mL	9 mL
2/3 tsp.	1/3 tsp.	calcium ascorbate powder	2 mL	4 mL
3 Tbsp.	1 Tbsp.	grated lemon rind	15 mL	45 mL
3 Tbsp.	1 Tbsp.	grated orange rind	15 mL	45 mL
1 cup	1/3 cup	soft margarine or butter	80 mL	240 mL
9	3	eggs	3	9
1 cup	1/3 cup	white sugar	80 mL	240 mL
1 cup	1/3 cup	hot tap water	80 mL	240 mL

1. Measure brown sugar into wide measuring cup. With same spoon, measure and add yeast.

2. Add cool or lukewarm water. Stir (lumps don't matter). Set in warm, draft-free place till needed (10 to 25 min).

3. Except for sugar, measure dry ingredients into plastic bowl. Mix well.

4. Beat eggs 5 min. Very gradually, add the sugar as you continue beating. Beat 7 more min.

5. Add soft margarine or butter, eggs beaten with sugar, and hot tap water to dry ingredients.

6. Immediately add yeast mixture and mix everything together very well with big spoon.

7. If some of the dry mixture won't mix in fairly easily, add a *little* more hot tap water.

8. Lay food wrap right over dough, touching surface. Cover bowl loosely. Set in warm, draft-free place.

9. After 30 min, dough should be about double in bulk. Peel off food wrap. Turn dough out on generously floured cookie sheet or board.

10. With generously floured hands, form dough into a long, even cylinder (one for each 12 rolls). With a sharp knife, cut the cylinder in half. Cut each of these halves in half, and then cut them into thirds so you have 12 equal-sized chunks of dough.

11. Roll the chunks of dough into balls and set them about 1 in. (2.5 cm) apart in an oiled bun pan. Spray with water.

12. Set rolls into oven and turn oven to its *lowest* setting. Leave 10 to 25 min.

13. When rolls have about doubled in size, turn oven up to 325°F (160°C).

14. From time of turning heat up, bake 15 to 20 min or until nicely browned. If tops start browning too much, protect with aluminum foil.

15. If desired, while still hot, put the following glaze on top: 8 parts sifted icing sugar mixed with 1 to 2 parts milk and vanilla extract to taste.

Cinnamon Rolls / *One bakery where I worked was known far and wide for its wonderful cinnamon rolls. With this recipe you can have a similar reputation.*

24 rolls	8 rolls		8 rolls	24 rolls
1-1/2 Tbsp.	1/2 Tbsp.	sugar	7 mL	21 mL
3 Tbsp.	1 Tbsp.	active dry or fast-rise yeast	15 mL	45 mL
3/4 cup	1/4 cup	cool or lukewarm water	60 mL	180 mL
6 cups	2 cups	all-purpose flour	480 mL	1440 mL
1-1/2 cup	1/2 cup	gluten flour	120 mL	360 mL
1-1/2 cup	1/2 cup	milk powder	120 mL	360 mL
3 tsp.	1 tsp.	salt or sea salt	5 mL	15 mL
2/3 tsp.	1/3 tsp.	calcium ascorbate powder	2 mL	4 mL
3 cups	1 cup	raisins (soak a few minutes if they're hard)	240 mL	720 mL
1-1/2 cups	1/2 cup	soft margarine or butter (or less or omit)	120 mL	360 mL
6	2	eggs, slightly beaten	2	6
1-1/2 cups	1/2 cup	hot tap water	120 mL	360 mL
1 cup	1/3 cup	soft margarine or butter (or less or more)	80 mL	240 mL
1-1/2 cups	1/2 cup	brown sugar (or less or more)	120 mL	360 mL
6 Tbsp.	2 Tbsp.	cinnamon (or less or more)	30 mL	90 mL

1. Measure sugar into wide measuring cup. With same spoon, measure and add yeast.

2. Add cool or lukewarm water. Stir (lumps don't matter). Set in warm, draft-free place till needed (10 to 25 min).

3. Measure dry ingredients into plastic bowl. Mix well.

4. Add margarine or butter, slightly beaten eggs, and hot tap water to dry ingredients.

5. Immediately add yeast mixture and mix everything together very well with big spoon.

6. If some of the dry mixture won't mix in fairly easily, add a *little* more hot tap water.

7. Lay food wrap right over dough, touching surface. Cover bowl loosely. Set in warm, draft-free place.

8. After 30 min, dough should be about double in bulk. Peel off food wrap. Turn dough out on generously floured cookie sheet or board.

9. With generously floured hands, pat dough (for each group of 8 rolls) into a rectangle about 10 in. by 16 in. (25 cm by 40 cm). Spread with the last three ingredients listed, stopping a bit short of the edges.

10. Starting with a long edge, roll up as for jellyroll. Seal the long end well.

11. With a sharp knife, cut the roll in half. Cut each of these halves in half, and then in half again so that you have eight cinnamon rolls.

12. Set rolls beside each other, cut sides up and barely touching, in an oiled spring form pan or bun pan.

13. Set pan into oven, with a cookie sheet underneath to catch any drips. Turn oven to its lowest setting. Leave 10 to 25 min.

14. When rolls have about doubled in bulk, turn oven up to 375°F (190°C).

15. From time of turning heat up, bake 45 to 55 min or until nicely browned. If tops or bottoms start browning too much, turn heat down to 325°F (160°C) and/or protect with aluminum foil.

Mother-in-Laws' Christmas Wreath / *This recipe is based on a combination of two — one from my friend Barbara Hehner's mother-in-law, Gertrude Hehner, and the other from my own dear mother-in-law, Bernice Schemenauer.*

3 wreaths	1 wreath		1 wreath	3 wreaths
1-1/2 Tbsp.	1/2 Tbsp.	brown sugar	7 mL	21 mL
3 Tbsp.	1 Tbsp.	active dry or fast-rise yeast	15 mL	45 mL
3/4 cup	1/4 cup	cool or lukewarm water	60 mL	180 mL
6 cups	2 cups	all-purpose flour	480 mL	1440 mL
1-1/2 cup	1/2 cup	gluten flour	120 mL	360 mL
1-1/2 cup	1/2 cup	milk powder	120 mL	360 mL
1-1/2 tsp.	1/2 tsp.	salt or sea salt	3 mL	9 mL
2/3 tsp.	1/3 tsp.	calcium ascorbate powder	2 mL	4 mL
3/4 cup	1/4 cup	sugar	60 mL	180 mL
2-1/4 cups	3/4 cup	raisins (soak a few minutes if they're hard)	180 mL	540 mL
3 cups	1 cup	candied fruit (cherries, pineapple, etc.)	240 mL	720 mL
3 tsp.	1 tsp.	crushed cardamon seed	5 mL	15 mL
3/4 cup	1/4 cup	soft margarine or butter	60 mL	180 mL
2-1/4 cups	3/4 cup	hot tap water	180 mL	540 mL
1 cup	1/3 cup	soft margarine or butter (or less or more)	80 mL	240 mL
1-1/2 cups	1/2 cup	brown sugar (or less or more)	120 mL	360 mL
6 Tbsp.	2 Tbsp.	cinnamon (or less or more)	30 mL	90 mL

1. Measure brown sugar into wide measuring cup. With same spoon, measure and add yeast.

2. Add cool or lukewarm water. Stir (lumps don't matter). Set in warm, draft-free place till needed (10 to 25 min).

3. Measure dry ingredients into plastic bowl. Mix well.

4. Add margarine or butter and hot tap water to dry ingredients.

5. Immediately add yeast mixture and mix everything together very well with big spoon.

6. If some of the dry mixture won't mix in fairly easily, add a *little* more hot tap water.

7. Lay food wrap right over dough, touching surface. Cover bowl loosely. Set in warm, draft-free place.

8. After 30 min, dough should be about double in bulk. Peel off food wrap. Turn dough out on generously floured cookie sheet or board.

9. With generously floured hands, press dough (for each wreath) into a rectangle about 8 in. by 18 in. (20 cm by 45 cm). Spread with the last three ingredients listed, stopping a bit short of the edges.

10. Starting with a long edge, roll up as for jellyroll. Seal the long end.

11. Carefully lift the roll onto an oiled cookie sheet. Curve it into a wreath, sealing the join well. With a sharp knife, make shallow cuts about 3 in. (7 cm) apart all around wreath. Spray with water.

12. Set wreath(s) into oven and turn to its lowest setting. Leave 10 to 25 min.

13. When dough is about double in size, turn oven up to 350°F (175°C).

14. From time of turning heat up, bake 30 to 40 min or till nicely browned. If the top or bottom start browning too much, turn heat down to 325°F (160°C) and/or protect with aluminum foil.

15. If desired, while still hot, put the following glaze on top: 8 parts sifted icing sugar mixed with 1 to 2 parts milk and vanilla extract to taste.

Pizza Neapolitan / *For a festive color combination, try topping this with pineapple, ham, and green peppers.*

3 medium	1 medium		1 medium	3 medium
3 tsp.	1 tsp.	sugar	5 mL	15 mL
2 Tbsp.	2 tsp.	active dry or fast-rise yeast	10 mL	30 mL
3/4 cup	1/4 cup	cool or lukewarm water	60 mL	180 mL
3-3/4 cup	1-1/4 cup	all-purpose flour	300 mL	900 mL
3/4 cup	1/4 cup	gluten flour	60 mL	180 mL
1-1/2 tsp.	1/2 tsp.	salt or sea salt	3 mL	9 mL
1/2 tsp.	1/4 tsp.	calcium ascorbate powder	1.5 mL	4.5 mL
1-1/2 cup	1/2 cup	hot tap water	120 mL	360 mL
6	2	medium tomatoes, peeled and sliced (or use tomato sauce spread about 1/4 in. [or 0.6 cm] thick on dough)	2	6
3	1	garlic clove(s), peeled and chopped	1	3
18 oz.	6 oz.	mozzarella cheese, thinly sliced	170 g	510 g
		any of the following according to taste: oregano, basil, pepper, pineapple chunks, chopped peppers, sliced mushrooms, cubed ham, sliced sausage, chopped bacon		

1. Measure sugar into wide measuring cup. With same spoon, measure and add yeast.

2. Add cool or lukewarm water. Stir (lumps don't matter). Set in warm, draft-free place till needed (10 to 25 min).

3. Measure dry ingredients into plastic bowl. Mix well.

4. Add hot tap water to dry ingredients.

5. Immediately add yeast mixture and mix everything together very well with big spoon.

6. If some of the dry mixture won't mix in fairly easily, add a *little* more hot tap water.

7. Lay food wrap right over dough, touching surface. Cover bowl loosely. Set in warm, draft-free place.

8. After 30 min, dough should be about double in bulk. Peel off food wrap. With generously floured hands, press (each pizza) into an oiled, medium-sized pizza pan. Or form it into a circle about 1/4 in. (0.6 cm) thick on an oiled baking sheet. In either case, build up the edges slightly.

9. Top with the tomatoes or tomato sauce. Then pile on the other ingredients. If using chopped bacon, you may wish to fry it for a few minutes first so it will be sure to get thoroughly cooked.

10. Bake at 425°F (218°C) for 25 to 30 min.

In the Middle Ages, Roman soldiers used flat unrisen cakes of bread called trenchers *as plates for cutting up meat. When the meat was gone, trenchers were eaten or thrown to the poor.*

SPECIAL BREADS 83

Judy's Alfalfa Sprout Bread / *This recipe is based on one given to me by our next-door neighbor and helpful friend, Judy Lynn Simpson. You can either buy the sprouts or grow them yourself. (See the Appendix.)*

3 loaves	1 loaf		1 loaf	3 loaves
1-1/2 Tbsp.	1/2 Tbsp.	sugar	7 mL	21 mL
3 Tbsp.	1 Tbsp.	active dry or fast-rise yeast	15 mL	45 mL
3/4 cup	1/4 cup	cool or lukewarm water	60 mL	180 mL
6 cups	2 cups	all-purpose flour (or equal parts all-purpose and wholewheat flour)	480 mL	1440 mL
1-1/2 cup	1/2 cup	gluten flour	120 mL	360 mL
1-1/2 cup	1/2 cup	cracked wheat (or less or omit)	120 mL	360 mL
1-1/2 cup	1/2 cup	milk powder	120 mL	360 mL
3 tsp.	1 tsp.	salt or sea salt	5 mL	15 mL
2/3 tsp.	1/3 tsp.	calcium ascorbate powder	2 mL	4 mL
4-1/2 cups	1-1/2 cup	alfalfa sprouts, washed and well dried with paper towels	360 mL	1080 mL
3/8 cup	1/8 cup	soft shortening or oil (or less or more)	30 mL	90 mL
3 cups	1 cup	hot tap water	240 mL	720 mL

1. Measure sugar into wide measuring cup. With same spoon, measure and add yeast.

2. Add cool or lukewarm water. Stir (lumps don't matter). Set in warm, draft-free place till needed (10 to 25 min).

3. Measure dry ingredients into plastic bowl. Make sure sprouts are thoroughly dry before you add them. Mix well.

4. Add shortening and hot tap water to dry ingredients.

5. Immediately add yeast mixture and mix everything together very well with big spoon.

6. If some of the dry mixture won't mix in fairly easily, add a *little* more hot tap water.

7. Lay food wrap right over dough, touching surface. Cover bowl loosely. Set in warm, draft-free place.

8. After 30 min, dough should be about double in bulk. Peel off food wrap. Turn dough out on generously floured cookie sheet or board.

9. With generously floured hands, form loaf (or loaves).

10. Brush off extra flour. Spray bottom and sides of loaf with water.

11. Oil loaf pan. Set loaf in pan and spray top with water.

12. If desired, sprinkle cracked wheat on top.

13. Set bread into oven and turn oven to its *lowest* setting. Leave 10 to 25 min.

14. When dough has risen 1 to 2 in. (2.5 to 5.0 cm) above top of pan, turn oven up to 400°F (200°C).

15. From time of turning heat up, bake 30 to 45 min or till sides and bottom are nicely browned.

16. If you slice this bread while it's still hot, it may seem too moist. However, once it's cooled, the texture is just right.

Sprouted Wheat Bread / Long ago, people learned to prevent scurvy by sprouting their wheat before using it to make bread. Not only is sprouted wheat bread highly nutritious. It also got rave reviews from the tasters. For a simple method of sprouting wheat, see the Appendix.

3 loaves	1 loaf		1 loaf	3 loaves
1-1/2 Tbsp.	1/2 Tbsp.	brown sugar	7 mL	21 mL
3 Tbsp.	1 Tbsp.	active dry or fast-rise yeast	15 mL	45 mL
3/4 cup	1/4 cup	cool or lukewarm water	60 mL	180 mL
3 cups	1 cup	all-purpose flour	240 mL	720 mL
3 cups	1 cup	wholewheat flour	240 mL	720 mL
1-1/2 cup	1/2 cup	gluten flour	120 mL	360 mL
1-1/2 cup	1/2 cup	milk powder	120 mL	360 mL
3 tsp.	1 tsp.	salt or sea salt	5 mL	15 mL
2/3 tsp.	1/3 tsp.	calcium ascorbate powder	2 mL	4 mL
4-1/2 cups	1-1/2 cup	young wheat sprouts, with shoots no longer than the grain itself	360 mL	1080 mL
3/8 cup	1/8 cup	soft shortening or oil (or less or more)	30 mL	90 mL
3/4 cup	1/4 cup	molasses or honey (or less or omit)	60 mL	180 mL
2 cups	2/3 cup	hot tap water	160 mL	480 mL

1. Use a blender or food mill to chop the wheat sprouts till they're about the consistency of coarse porridge. (You can leave some of them whole if you like. However, they tend to become somewhat hard when baked in the bread.)

2. Measure brown sugar into wide measuring cup. With same spoon, measure and add yeast.

3. Add cool or lukewarm water. Stir (lumps don't matter). Set in warm, draft-free place till needed (10 to 25 min).

4. Measure dry ingredients into plastic bowl. Mix well.

5. Add shortening, molasses or honey, and hot tap water to dry ingredients.

6. Immediately add yeast mixture and mix everything together very well with big spoon.

7. If some of the dry mixture won't mix in fairly easily, add a *little* more hot tap water.

8. Lay food wrap right over dough, touching surface. Cover bowl loosely. Set in warm, draft-free place.

9. After 30 min, dough should be about double in bulk. Peel off food wrap. Turn dough out on generously floured cookie sheet or board.

10. With generously floured hands, form loaf (or loaves).

11. Brush off extra flour. Spray bottom and sides of loaf with water.

12. Oil loaf pan. Set loaf in pan and spray top with water.

13. If desired, sprinkle cracked wheat on top.

14. Set bread into oven and turn oven to its *lowest* setting. Leave 10 to 25 min.

15. When dough has risen 1 to 2 in. (2.5 to 5.0 cm) above top of pan, turn oven up to 400°F (200°C).

16. From time of turning heat up, bake 30 to 45 min or till sides and bottom are nicely browned.

French-style Bread / Good French-style bread is usually baked in the presence of steam. The proper conditions are hard to achieve in the home oven. However, I've developed a method that works amazingly well, and is simpler and safer than most.

6 loaves	2 loaves		2 loaves	6 loaves
1-1/2 Tbsp.	1/2 Tbsp.	sugar	7 mL	21 mL
3 Tbsp.	1 Tbsp.	active dry or fast-rise yeast	15 mL	45 mL
3/4 cup	1/4 cup	cool or lukewarm water	60 mL	180 mL
6 cups	2 cups	all-purpose flour (or equal parts all-purpose and wholewheat flour)	480 mL	1440 mL
1-1/2 cup	1/2 cup	gluten flour	120 mL	360 mL
1-1/2 cup	1/2 cup	wheat germ (or less or omit)	120 mL	360 mL
3/8 cup	1/8 cup	soy flour (or less or omit)	30 mL	90 mL
3 tsp.	1 tsp.	salt or sea salt	5 mL	15 mL
2/3 tsp.	1/3 tsp.	calcium ascorbate powder	2 mL	4 mL
3 cups	1 cup	hot tap water	240 mL	720 mL

1. Measure sugar into wide measuring cup. With same spoon, measure and add yeast.

2. Add cool or lukewarm water. Stir (lumps don't matter). Set in warm, draft-free place till needed (10 to 25 min).

3. Measure dry ingredients into plastic bowl. Mix well.

4. Add hot tap water to dry ingredients.

5. Immediately add yeast mixture and mix everything together very well with big spoon.

6. If some of the dry mixture won't mix in fairly easily, add a *little* more hot tap water.

7. Lay food wrap right over dough touching surface. Cover bowl loosely. Set in warm, draft-free place.

8. After 30 min, dough should be about double in bulk. Peel off food wrap. Turn dough out on generously floured cookie sheet or board.

9. With generously floured hands, form long skinny loaves.

10. Brush off extra flour. Spray bottoms and sides of loaves with water.

11. Put quarry tiles on oven rack (see page 20). For each loaf, oil an area of tiles somewhat bigger than the loaf. Set the loaves directly on the tiles.

12. Turn oven to its *lowest* setting. Leave loaves 20 to 30 min, or until more than doubled in size. Then turn heat up to 470°F (240°C).

13. When oven has reached this temperature, use a plant mister to spray loaves and tiles generously with water. As you spray hot tiles, dramatic bursts of steam will rise. This steam is what gives French-style bread its crustiness and stretchy texture. (Be careful not to burn yourself.)

14. Continue baking at 470°F (240°C). Every 5 min or so, spray loaves and tiles again. Bake till sides and bottom are the desired shade of brown.

Teresa Macchiusi's Italian Bread / *This bread is based on a recipe from the mother of longtime friend Mary Macchiusi. Because of the slow baking — like what takes place in an old-fashioned Italian outdoor oven — this bread takes longer than most in this book. But it's worth it!*

3 loaves	1 loaf		1 loaf	3 loaves
1-1/2 Tbsp.	1/2 Tbsp.	sugar	7 mL	21 mL
3 Tbsp.	1 Tbsp.	active dry or fast-rise yeast	15 mL	45 mL
3/4 cup	1/4 cup	cool or lukewarm water	60 mL	180 mL
6 cups	2 cups	all-purpose flour (or equal parts all-purpose and wholewheat flour)	480 mL	1440 mL
1-1/2 cup	1/2 cup	gluten flour	120 mL	360 mL
3 tsp.	1 tsp.	salt or sea salt	5 mL	15 mL
2/3 tsp.	1/3 tsp.	calcium ascorbate powder	2 mL	4 mL
3 cups	1 cup	hot tap water	240 mL	720 mL

1. Measure sugar into wide measuring cup. With same spoon, measure and add yeast.

2. Add cool or lukewarm water. Stir (lumps don't matter). Set in warm, draft-free place till needed (10 to 25 min).

3. Measure dry ingredients into plastic bowl. Mix well.

4. Add hot tap water to dry ingredients.

5. Immediately add yeast mixture and mix everything together very well with big spoon.

6. If some of the dry mixture won't mix in fairly easily, add a *little* more hot tap water.

7. Lay food wrap right over dough, touching surface. Cover bowl loosely. Set in warm, draft-free place.

8. After 30 min, dough should be about double in bulk. Peel off food wrap. Turn dough out on generously floured cookie sheet or board.

9. With generously floured hands, form loaf (or loaves).

10. Brush off extra flour. Spray bottom and sides of loaf with water.

11. Oil a sheet of aluminum foil at least twice as large as the loaf. Lay foil on oven rack and set loaf directly on it. Spray with water.

12. If desired, sprinkle sesame seeds on top.

13. Turn oven to its *lowest* setting. Leave bread 20 to 30 min, or until more than doubled in size. Then turn heat up to 400°F (200°C).

14. After 15 min, lower heat to 300°F (150°C) and continue baking about one hour, or till sides and bottom are nicely browned.

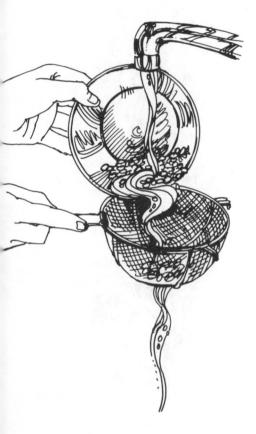

Appendix

Growing Sprouts for Sprout Breads

1. Wheat, rye, or alfalfa sprouts work well in breads. About 1/2 cup unsprouted seeds will yield about 4 cups sprouts.

2. Wash seeds and soak overnight in 4 times as much warm water as seeds. Drain. (The soaking water is nutritious and can be added to soups or stews.)

3. Put the seeds in a wide-bottomed enamel, china, plastic, glass, or unglazed pottery container, spreading them evenly.

4. Soak a couple of paper towels in water, wring out slightly, and lay on top of seeds. Cover and leave in a convenient place.

5. About 4 hours later, remove paper towels. Rinse seeds with water, draining them into a strainer.

6. Tap the seeds back into the sprouting container. Put the wet paper towels back on (rewet them if they've dried out). Cover container.

7. Repeat the rinsing process 3 or 4 times a day. After 5 or 6 days, your sprouts should be ready to use.

Note: The above method can be used for sprouting a wide variety of seeds and beans; for example, lentils, peas, radish seeds, mung beans, navy beans, pinto beans. However, these are more often used in salads and for cooking rather than in breadbaking.

Index

Give BREADSPEED to your family and friends!

Send $8.95 per copy plus $1.00 per copy for mailing. On orders of 3 or more books, mailing costs are included in the $8.95 per book price. Send orders to:

Order Dept.
Farland Press Inc.
92 Caines Ave.
Willowdale, Ontario
Canada, M2R 2L3

(For orders of 20 or more, send for our discount price list.)

ORDER FORM

Please send me _____ copies of BREADSPEED. I enclose $8.95 per book plus $1.00 each for mailing if ordering 1 or 2 books. Total enclosed is $_____.

Name _____

Apartment Number _____

Street _____

City _____

Province/State _____

Country _____

Postal Code _____

Make money order or cheque payable to Farland Press Inc.
